Battleground Europe
BATTLE OF THE BULGE

SAINT VITH
106TH US INFANTRY DIVISION

Battleground Europe
BATTLE OF THE BULGE

SAINT VITH
106TH US INFANTRY DIVISION

Michael Tolhurst

LEO COOPER

COMBINED PUBLISHING
Pennsylvania

First published in 1999 by
LEO COOPER
an imprint of
Pen & Sword Books Limited
47 Church Street, Barnsley, South Yorkshire S70 2AS

Copyright © Mike Tolhurst

ISBN 0 85052 665 5

A CIP catalogue record of this book is available
from the British Library

Printed by Redwood Books Limited
Trowbridge, Wiltshire

*For up-to-date information on other titles produced under the Leo Cooper imprint,
please telephone or write to:*

Pen & Sword Books Ltd, FREEPOST, 47 Church Street
Barnsley, South Yorkshire S70 2AS
Telephone 01226 734222

Published under license in the United States of America by

COMBINED PUBLISHING

ISBN 1-58097-016-8

For information, address:
COMBINED PUBLISHING
P.O. Box 307
Conshohocken, PA 19428
E-Mail: combined@dca.net
Web: www.combinedpublishing.com
Orders: 1-800-418-6065

*Cataloging in Publication Data available from the Library of
Congress*

CONTENTS

FOREWORD

Mike Tolhurst, author, and Pen & Sword Books Ltd have done an excellent job in this military history guide covering the actions of the 106th Infantry Division during the 'Battle of the Bulge' in *Battleground St Vith*.

I met Mike, through correspondence, in the early '90s. He had been, and has been since, vacationing in the Ardennes area. He understands the 106th Infantry Division's positions as well as any person I have ever met. His intimate knowledge of the area, gleaned over the years, makes him a good authority and a great choice for authoring such a fine history guide as *Battleground St Vith*.

St Vith was the primary objective for the Germans as they broke through the defences of the 106th Infantry Division, entrenched along the Schnee Eifel, 16th December 1944. St Vith, a transportation hub with a railroad and five main roads, was a major objective in the German Offensive time-table. Their Battle Orders dictated that it should be taken on the first day of battle. Had this been achieved their advance to the Meuse River would have been open. The Germans never seized St Vith until days later. Too much time, too many resources had been wasted because of the stubborn resistance of the 106th Infantry Division.

What would have happened at Bastogne had those German troops, held up at St Vith, been available for use in the fight for that town? The German General Staff realized that once their timetable had been thrown out at St Vith they would be unable to get back on schedule.

Mike Tolhurst's use of veterans' accounts makes his history very personal. Here you will read how it was from the soldiers that fought the battle. His intimate knowledge of the territory is invaluable to those who wish to browse the area, to feel and sense the happenings of those times. When you take the trails and roads through the battle area, you will, like me, wonder how the war was ever fought there. It is a fantastically beautiful country. It seems a pity that this land was raped by war.

One of my comrades, Dale Carver, a 2nd Lieutenant, an Ammunition and Pioneer Platoon Leader in the Headquarters Company, Third Battalion, 424th Infantry Regiment, 106th Infantry Division, a Silver Star recipient, wrote in his book of poems the following:

ARDENNES

Majestic firs, snow laden,
in rank and file stand.
A man amid the pungent boughs

Needled boughs, star laden,
pressed by a grimy hand –
ice against an anguished brow,
alone in a troubled land.

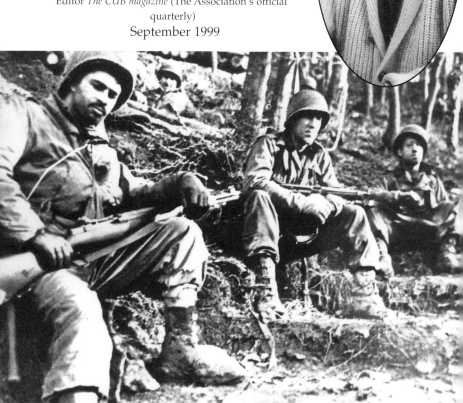

As I read this I see a lonely rifleman, cold and hungry and in a strange land.

John Kline

M Company, 423rd Infantry WWII
Sergeant heavy machine gun squad leader
Past-President 106th Infantry Division Association
Editor *The CUB magazine* (The Association's official
quarterly)
September 1999

INTRODUCTION

The purpose of this book is not to confuse the reader with the many complexities arising from the 'Battle of the Bulge' (December 1944 - January 1945), nor get involved with the politics or controversial decisions made, but to give an idea, basically, how the battle came about and, because of the vastness of the battleground area, to concentrate on one portion of it.

The battle was the biggest pitched engagement of the Western Front, involving over one million men. It was Hitler's last desperate gamble and was probably one of the most astonishing episodes of World War II, also the most controversial. It shook the Western Alliance, incredible

Protecting Germany's westward approaches from Holland to Switzerland was the much vaunted Siegfried Line or West Wall. Propaganda sold the idea that it would present an impregnable barrier to the Allies. In September 1944, Montgomery's plan to jump around Germany's defences at Arnhem had failed.

Concrete pillboxes and machine gun posts, with overlapping fields of fire were situated between 200 and 400 yards behind the 'dragon's teeth' of the Siegfried Line. These defences began to be breached in September – the furthest penetration being in the area of the Ardennes.

confusion reigned, and it finally broke the Germans.

It was a time of triumph and at the same time deep national humiliation, owing to the fact that the Americans suffered the largest mass surrender or reversal of arms since (with the exception of Bataan 1942) the Civil War (1861-66).

In the beginning of December 1944 it seemed to the Allies that the Germans were on their last legs. They had been under constant pressure since the D-Day landings six months previously, and had been chased back into their own country. The end was in sight. 'Home for Christmas,' or at the latest New Year, was on the lips of the fighting men.

In September the Allies had forged ahead and had come up hard against the 'Westwall' or 'Siegfried Line' as it was called. Bitter fighting had found the Allied troops in amongst this formidable obstacle. The long over-stretched supply routes, originating from the Normandy beaches, and the very recently captured port of Antwerp, were now beginning to slow. It was decided to stop the offensive for the winter, straighten the line and allow the much-needed supplies to catch up.

One such part of the 'Westwall' was deep in the Belgian

German prisoners stream back through the anti-tank obstacles of the Siegfried Line in September 1944.

GIs trying to get comfortable among the forests of the Ardennes as the winter of 1944 draws in.

Ardennes on the border with Germany. In this area the furthest penetration into Germany had been made. Here on the German side lies a high ridge running north to south. This mass of volcanic hills forms part of what the Germans call the Eifel Region and stretches from Monschau in the north down to the River Moselle in the south. Almost in the centre of this, opposite the Belgian town of St Vith, is the highest portion of this ridge line and is called the 'Schnee Eifel' (Snow Eifel). Heavy fighting in September/October had pushed the Germans off the Schnee Eifel and it was now occupied by US troops.

Long famed for its natural beauty and charm, the Ardennes had been popular with holiday makers long before the war. The countryside is criss-crossed with ridges, ravines and rivers, and, in some places, gentle rolling hills. The roads are sparse and narrow, generally following the tracks of the rivers. Everywhere is covered with woods, much of it pine, and in some places quite impenetrable. Because of the nature of the land it was considered a safe area. It became known among the troops as the 'Ghost Front', where US Divisions could be sent to acclimatize themselves ready for the coming offensives, or where units, which had already seen heavy combat, could go for a rest and regroup.

Patrolling seemed the only hazard to life; both sides sent out patrols and each reported back that the opposition was light and that all was quiet. The troops made themselves as comfortable as possible, knowing that winter was upon them. All the many small villages that are dotted around the region were occupied by various headquarters and rear echelon staff. The front-line troops made what they could out of the 'Westwall' bunkers, captured in September, or lined and covered their exposed foxholes with whatever they could find. As the young GIs quipped: 'Nothing ever happens in the Awful Eifel'. They were in for a surprise.

On the German side plans were afoot. Already in September 1944, in the midst of apparent defeat, Hitler had decided on one last-ditch offensive. He knew the Allied alliance was shaky. The British and American Generals were always disagreeing about which way the war should go. He

German concrete bunker on top of Schnee Eifel showing heavy damage. These positions were occupied by Americans prior to the German attack in December 1944.

decided that, if he could split the two factions there might be a chance he could sue for peace, on his terms.

Hitler's plan was simple. In the north, under old Party bully boy and now SS General, Sepp Dietrich, and his Sixth SS Panzer Army would charge through between Monschau and the Losheim Gap (a natural break in the otherwise hilly terrain which gave easier east-west access) and head straight for Antwerp. This would then force a wedge between the British and American Armies. In the centre, General von Manteuffel's Fifth Panzer Army was to capture the two major rail and road centres at St Vith and Bastogne deep in the Ardennes and then drive on to Brussels. Finally, the Seventh Army, under General Brandenberger to the south, was to provide flanking protection for the two northern attacks.

But before Manteuffel could get to St Vith and Bastogne he would have to eliminate this furthest penetration, or salient, which by this time was being held by the green and untried US 106th Division. So under complete secrecy and unknown to the Allies, the Germans prepared and massed their armies behind the Eifel Region in the German homeland. To stop them was the greenest, youngest (average age was 22) division in the whole of the Allied Armies in Europe that December.

A tragedy was in the making.

The Purpose of the Guide

To cover the site of America's greatest military defeat of WWII. Nowhere in the world is there a battlefield like this, left basically as it was in 1945

This guide will enable you to tour this particular portion of the front, see the now celebrated landmarks and ground that both Germans and American alike fought so hard over and where the ill-fated 106th Division would succumb to that onslaught in that terrible winter of December 1944. Here the informed reader can examine the foxholes in which the GIs fought; the German gunpits; see the place where thousands of Americans surrendered, all not much changed in half a century.

Remember – this is a 'hands on' guide. – BRING YOUR WELLIES! (Rubber boots).

GLOSSARY

AA	**Anti Aircraft**
AD	**Armored Division**
	Approx 10,937 men Divided into 3 sections:
	Combat Command A (CCA)
	Combat Command B (CCB)
	Combat Command R (CCR)
	(Reserve)
AIB	**Armored Infantry Battalion**
	(Fully mechanized infantry usually carried in half tracks)
AT	**Anti-Tank**
BATT	**Battalion** (Approx 871 men)
BAZOOKA	American hand held anti-tank rocket.
CAV	**Cavalry** (A small highly mechanized group used for reconnaissance and screening. Organized into 'Troops', containing M5 light Stuart tanks, M8 Armoured Cars and Jeeps.

CP	**Command Post** or Headquarters
CO	**Company** (Approx 193 men)
ENG	**Combat Engineer Battalion** (Approx 647 men). Attached to a Division.
DIV	**Division** (Approx 14,253 men with 2,012 vehicles)
FAB	**Field Artillery Battalion** (Approx 500 men). Split into three Batteries.

GI	**Government Issue** (Anything issued by the American Government, including men!
HETZER	**German tank destroyer**, mounting a 75mm PaK 39 (L/48) gun. Designed to defend infantry against enemy armour. Crew of four. Speed 26 mph.

INF	**Infantry**
MED	**Medical** as in Medical Battalion (Approx 465 men)
M8	**American Armoured Car**. 6 wheels, mounting a 37mm gun. 4 crew, max speed 56 mph.

In the hands of new masters an armoured car – M8.

PANZER	**German for Armour** (Eg Tank). Panzergrenadier being mechanized infantry.
PURPLE HEART	**American medal** (Award) for being wounded in action.

REGT	**Regiment** United States (Approx 3118 men)
SHERMAN	**M4 standard American tank** used by every Allied nation. Crew of 5, with a speed of 24 - 29 mph. There were many different variants, but most were armed with either a 75mm or 76mm gun.

STURMGESCHÜTZ	**German self-propelled 75mm /105mm** assault gun. Crew of 4, Usually arranged in assault gun battalions, each with 3 batteries containing 6 vehicles. But these were later enlarged into army assault artillery brigades, with anything up to 45 assault guns and a small infantry component.
TD	**Tank destroyer**. (Either the self-propelled type, as in the M10 tank destroyer, this mounted a 3 inch gun, had a max speed of 30 mph with a crew of 5. Or the towed type, which was a 3 inch field gun, drawn by a vehicle.

VGD	**Volksgrenadier Division**. Came into being late in the war. Made up of Naval/Airforce fillers mixed with regular army. (A match for any Allied division).
6X6	**GMC cargo truck**. A general utility truck that was the workhorse of the American army.

88	**German 88mm gun**, much feared by the Allies. It was mounted on Tiger tanks, or as a field piece in either the ground or anti-aircraft role.

CHAPTER ONE

THE GOLDEN LIONS
(1943-1944)
Birth of a Division

The 106th Infantry Division was
officially activated in the United States
15 March 1943. It was just one of the
ninety new formations intended for
overseas service as the US Army
continued to swell to meet its
commitments in a world conflict,
which was devouring men at an
ever increasing rate. American
troops were 'blooded' in the
European theatre with the landings
in North Africa, Operation 'Torch'
and the later clashes with Rommel's
Afrika Korps. The training and battle tactics
were not up to standard and as a consequence the American
elements of the Anglo-American 1st Army suffered at the
Battle of Kasserine Pass in January 1943. It took the combined
efforts of Patton and Bradley to transform the US 2nd Corps
into a first rate fighting force. With the invasion of Europe
through Sicily and Italy, and the proposed Second Front in
northern Europe on the horizon, raising and training of
infantry divisions was high on the list of priorities. The 106th
were due for a rigorous training that would equip them to
face the most efficient fighting machine the world had seen
to date – the German army.

* * * *

Midday on Monday 15 March, 1943. A large limousine
pulled up in front of No 2 Outdoor Theatre at Fort Jackson,

19

South Carolina. Alighting from the car was the Honorable Olin D. Johnston, Governor of that State. Along with other dignitaries he took his place on the stage in front of the massed ranks furnished from the parent organization, the 80th Infantry Division. The Divisional Chaplain, Major John A. Dunn, pronounced the Invocation, followed by the Adjutant General, Lieutenant-Colonel Frank I. Agule, who read the official birth certificate – the War Department order for the activation of the 106th Infantry Division. On completion of the speeches, Master Sergeant Jay G. Bower – acting as the representative of the parent 80th Infantry Division – summoned from the ranks of the 422nd Infantry Regiment Private Francis A.Younkin, one of the youngest new recruits. To this new, raw recruit, Sergeant Bower handed over the National Colours entrusting its keeping to the new division. More speeches, and then General Jones gives a brief message to his command ending with the statement,

'In your hands is held the opportunity to fashion an instrument which will demonstrate to the world that our way of life develops men superior to any other'.

The ceremony came to an end with the Benediction, after which the men were dismissed. The 106th Infantry Division was now officially on the rolls of the Army and the United States.

The idea of these new divisions was to form a nucleus of already well-experienced men and build the newly drafted recruits around them, keep them together so that they would form a bonded team and train them well. The end product would have then been through every conceivable task that would be expected of an infantry division, 'except come under real fire from an enemy'.

The Divisional Commander was Major General Alan W. Jones; Assistant Commander was Brigadier General Herbert T Perrin; and the Division's Artillery Commander was Brigadier General Leo T McMahon.

Basic training began on 29 March, 1943, followed on 12 July by Unit training. From October 1943 to January 1944 more training but this time on a regimental and divisional level. This was held in central South Carolina, in the field. For the first time men learned how to cope with mud and freezing rain.

From January to March 1944 the Division took part in gruelling manoeuvres in Tennessee. The area took up the best part of the centre of that state. These were under realistic battlefield conditions. Along with other units, the 106th took part in daily manoeuvres, learning all the skills the Army had to offer them. Even the weather was terrible, and unknown to the men at that time, very similar to what they would be experiencing in the Ardennes – nine months later.

General Jones went on to say,

Major General Alan Jones

'The months training there were extremely beneficial to us and we came out of Tennessee a trained division, with much experience and great promise. We learned how to get our trucks through mud and country roads, how to make the most of supper eaten at night in the rain without light, how to wear mosquito headnets in a snow storm, we learned through days and nights of discomfort how best to take care of ourselves and, best of all, we learned that, as a fighting division, we were better than most.'

To the men of the division at that time, one thing will always be remembered. It became fondly regarded as the secret weapon of the 106th. This was the 'Bag Lunch – M1'. There were quite a few times when the men could not get back to the mess halls due to different tactical situations during exercises. So the cooks would prepare each man a bag meal. These were quite appetizing at first, but soon drifted into boring hastily thrown-together sandwiches, containing who

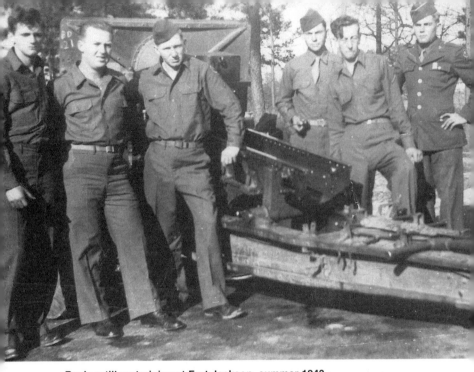

Basic artillery training at Fort Jackson, summer 1943.

Anti-Tank Company, 422nd Infantry Regiment, Mess Hall Fort Jackson

Men of the 589th Field Artillery during live firing practise with their 105mm howitzers, Camp Atterbury, Spring 1944.

Front centre: T/4 Randolph C. Pierson, 589th FA Fire Direction Center VCO. *Clockwise left to right*: T/4 Ruona, 590th FAB Survey Sergeant and members of his crew – Privates Slack, Fienberg and Kaufman.

knows what ! One such filler was peanut butter mixed with grape jam. After living in the field for days on end the men would eat anything. Well, almost!

The Division passed out as average and was now at the peak of readiness; the men and officers were working well together. They were moved to Camp Atterbury Indiana, where they hoped new equipment would arrive before going overseas. Then came the savage blow. The War Department's axe fell and the authorities drafted just over half of these men as replacements to other depleted fighting units. The Division was being stripped of its highly trained personnel. In their place came young men from all different branches of the Army and Airforce; some were volunteers for the infantry and some were not. The 106th did not recover from this drainage of experienced men. The new men were not to blame. It was the way the War Department went about things. It would take months and months to get the Division back up to scratch, but there just was not the time.

John Hillard Dunn remembers joining Company H (Heavy Weapons) of the 423rd at Camp Atterbury:

> 'I was instructed to report to my squad leader. I walked up to him in the barracks and said: "Private Dunn reporting." And with my face growing red, I added, "I think I ought to tell you, Sergeant, that I don't know a damned thing about an 81-MM mortar." He turned to me and replied, "Don't worry, Mac, You ain't got a thing on me. I don't either. I've been a mess sergeant in Fort Benning for ten years."

The days at Camp Atterbury were hard with much training.

Chow line – men of 422nd Infantry Regiment at Camp Atterbury.

In between training, leave was granted to the nearby places, such as Indianapolis and Columbus. The division took part in many events during their stay there. A demonstration exercise lasting two days on 19 and 20 May, for the delegation of the Hoosier State Press Association, another demonstration on 3 June for the Under-Secretary of War Robert P Patterson and an Infantry Day exercise on 15 June for more than 5,000 visitors. On the 4th July 1944 the 106th took part in Independence Day Parades at Indianapolis and Cleveland simultaneously. All these schemes made a welcomed break from the normal routine. During their stay at Atterbury the *Cub* newspaper went into full swing. It had been started during the Tennessee man-

Field HQ, Anti-Tank Company, 422nd Infantry Regiment, 1st Sergeant Widmyer operating a radio.

eouvres. It still exists today as a quarterly news magazine. The editor at present is John Kline, who is totally dedicated to his work and does a superb job. He is just but one of the many heroes of the 106th.

At Camp Atterbury, Colonel Cavender called in Ivan Long, a Lieutenant, and offered him the Intelligence and Recon Platoon. 'At this point' he said, 'I was unaware of its function. Later, having completed the Army Ground Force Test we came out on top. Out of a possible 1,000 we had a test score of 999.8. One gas can was not completely filled.'

In September the Division moved by rail to Camp Myles Standish at Taunton, Massachusetts. This camp was a well-

Happy days for the men of 422nd Infantry Regiment – camp fire at Camp Atterbury. Corporal William Supko (later Staff Sergeant) submits to Field Bath-Foot Care from the Medic (in background).

Men of 81st Engineer Combat Battalion cleaning their weapons after firing on Camp Atterbury rifle range. *Left to right*: Agostini, Gallatin, Hetic and Sullivan.

Men of Company A, 81st Engineer Battalion, jumping from a tower during combat swimming training at Camp Atterbury.

known staging area before going overseas and secrecy was the word.

Glen Hartlieb, Service Company 592nd FAB recalls the day he left to go overseas:

'I well remember the day I left Myles Standish. It was 11 November, 1944, raining very hard, I was standing in the rain with all my gear on my back waiting to board the ship. This only added to my misery as I was less than enchanted by the thought of going up that gangplank. A short time later I boarded the ship and was on my way. The next day almost everyone got sick after running into a storm. I won't go into details on that but I found I had picked the wrong bunk when I reached my compartment. The bunks were five high and I had the centre. I should have been on top.'

Elements of the 106th Infantry Division aboard the *Aquitania*, October 1944.

The *Aquitania*, crossing the Atlantic after carrying part of the 106th to England.

The USCGS *Wakefield* (formerly the *Manhattan*). As a troopship she was carrying six times more passengers than she had originally been designed to carry. For the majority of men of the 106th it proved to be a new experience – as they encountered heavy weather.

The 106th shipped out in October-November 1944 and headed for England. After the proverbial coffee and doughnuts, the troops were packed on one time stately ships such as the *Queen Elizabeth* and *Aquitania*. One of these magnificent ships was the ex-United States Lines *Manhattan*. Now assigned as a troop carrier and renamed USCGS *Wakefield*, crewed by US Coastguards. Jammed packed into their assigned mess-decks the men were excited at the great adventure ahead of them. The *Wakefield*, like many troopships was carrying six times more passengers than they were ever designed to carry. Men were crammed into bunks five high, made of canvas wrapped around tubular frames. Mae Wests had to be worn at all times other than when sleeping. It was a rough crossing and to add to the gut-wrenching corkscrew motion the ship was travelling at full speed zig-zagging against U-boat threats. Not surprisingly the novelty of being at sea for the first time soon wore off. Meals were served twice a day, the queue stretched nearly the length of the ship which meant over an hour's wait for those whose stomachs were strong enough. Most meals consisted of mutton stew. The heads (toilets) were an experience in themselves, just a simple trough containing water and waste. John M. Roberts of the 592nd Field Artillery Battalion wrote 'You never sat on one of the holes at the end. As the water hit the wall at the end of the trough, the water (and whatever was in the water) splashed and sloshed up through the holes'.

On arrival in England they were billeted around the areas of Oxford and Gloucester. A little more training was introduced, but the time was chiefly spent drawing vehicles and equipment. This was how the 106th Infantry Division started its short, tragic life.

It was not long before orders were received. The Division sailed from Liverpool, Southampton and Weymouth on 1 December and spent three long dreary days bobbing about in the English Channel unable to land because of the terrible weather. Finally they docked at Le Havre and Rouen in France and went straight into bivouac in open fields deep in mud and with constant drizzle.

Le Havre in the autumn of 1944. It was here that the 106th landed and were camped before moving out for their place in the line.

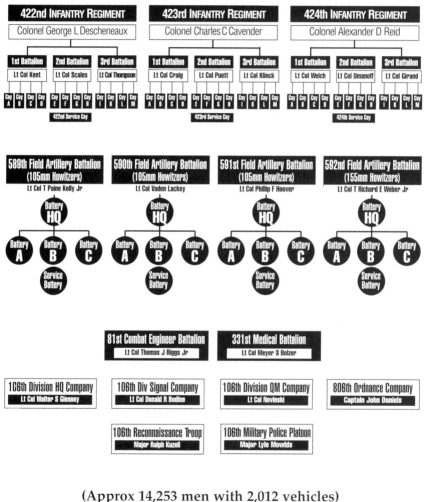

106th Infantry Division

Major General Alan W Jones *Commanding*

Brigadier General Herbert T Perrin *Assistant Commanding*

Brigadier General Leo T McMahon *Commanding Artillery*

Colonel Malin Craig Jr *Artillery Executive*

422nd INFANTRY REGIMENT
Colonel George L Descheneaux

1st Battalion Lt Col Kent — Coy A, Coy B, Coy C, Coy D
2nd Battalion Lt Col Scales — Coy E, Coy F, Coy G, Coy H
3rd Battalion Lt Col Thompson — Coy I, Coy K, Coy L, Coy M
422nd Service Coy

423rd INFANTRY REGIMENT
Colonel Charles C Cavender

1st Battalion Lt Col Craig — Coy A, Coy B, Coy C, Coy D
2nd Battalion Lt Col Puett — Coy E, Coy F, Coy G, Coy H
3rd Battalion Lt Col Klinck — Coy I, Coy K, Coy L, Coy M
423rd Service Coy

424th INFANTRY REGIMENT
Colonel Alexander D Reid

1st Battalion Lt Col Welch — Coy A, Coy B, Coy C, Coy D
2nd Battalion Lt Col Umanoff — Coy E, Coy F, Coy G, Coy H
3rd Battalion Lt Col Girand — Coy I, Coy K, Coy L, Coy M
424th Service Coy

589th Field Artillery Battalion (105mm Howitzers)
Lt Col T Paine Kelly Jr
Battery HQ — Battery A, Battery B, Battery C, Service Battery

590th Field Artillery Battalion (105mm Howitzers)
Lt Col Vaden Lackey
Battery HQ — Battery A, Battery B, Battery C, Service Battery

591st Field Artillery Battalion (105mm Howitzers)
Lt Col Phillip F Hoover
Battery HQ — Battery A, Battery B, Battery C, Service Battery

592nd Field Artillery Battalion (155mm Howitzers)
Lt Col T Richard E Weber Jr
Battery HQ — Battery A, Battery B, Battery C, Service Battery

81st Combat Engineer Battalion
Lt Col Thomas J Riggs Jr

331st Medical Battalion
Lt Col Meyer S Belzer

106th Division HQ Company Lt Col Walter S Glenney

106th Div Signal Company Lt Col Donald R Bodine

106th Division QM Company Lt Col Novinski

806th Ordnance Company Captain John Daniels

106th Reconnaissance Troop Major Ralph Kuzell

106th Military Police Platoon Major Lyle Mowlds

(Approx 14,253 men with 2,012 vehicles)

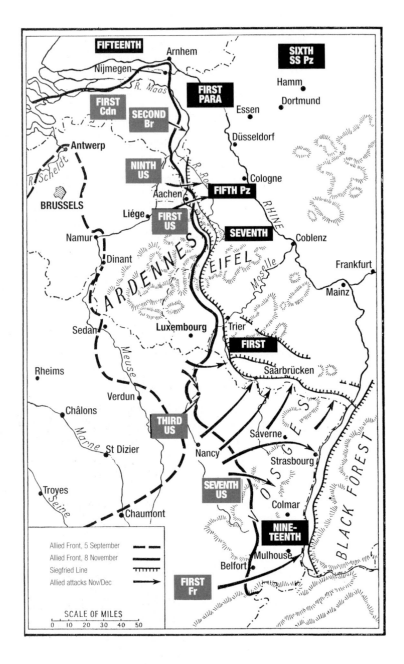

Situation map. By the beginning of December 1944 the German armies had been pushed back to their border and, in some places, the Siegfried Line had been penetrated.

CHAPTER TWO

INTO THE LINE
Arrival in Belgium and the 'Ghost' Front
December 1944

Instructions arrived on 6 December, 1944, that the Division was to head for the St Vith region of Belgium. Upon arrival they were to relieve the US 2nd Inf Div. The trucks began to roll; it was a miserable long trip, being bounced about, soaking wet through the ever-present rain and it was getting colder. It took two days before the long column of open vehicles reached their destination.

Due to the constant transportation and the inability to change into dry clothing a number of men were going down with various illnesses. Wags among the GIs began to call themselves 'The Hungry and Sick' a pun on the 106th Division's number. The men accepted this new-found name and laughed and joked about it among themselves. But woe

It was a long miserable journey to the front for the 106th Infantry Division. Vehicles of the 589th Field Artillery Battalion halt for a break near St Vith 8 or 9 December 1944.

St Vith 9 November, 1944, a quiet sector of the front. General Dwight D. Eisenhower with Major-General Troy H. Middleton, commander of VIII Corps.

betide any outsider calling them this. For in a relatively new division the men had already achieved a sense of pride and new-found comradeship.

Orders from General Troy Middleton, VIII Corps Commander, whose area the Golden Lions had joined, were to simply take over from the now leaving 2nd Infantry Division, man for man, gun for gun.

The Supply Officer, Charles Walsh of the 592nd Field Artillery Battalion recalls:

'We were a medium Field Artillery Battalion with full track prime movers pulling 155mm Howitzers. Our destination was the front lines near St Vith, Belgium. We were to relieve the Second Division. Our march to St Vith was to be three days. The column moved out at 35mph which, needless to say, caused many problems with our steel-track prime movers. The 592 F.A. Maintenance crew battled the 18 tractors for three days and three nights around the clock, replacing bogey wheels and one complete tractor, that had been in an accident coming down the mountain. The Battalion Maintenance crew consisted of two maintenance trucks and a battalion wrecker, and six men. They did a fantastic job getting the battalion up into the line at Laudesfeld without the assistance of the Division Ordnance Company that was supposed to be supporting them. The Ordnance Company made the trip on schedule with all their tools still packed in the shipping cartons the way they left the States.'

Leading elements arrived in the St Vith area early afternoon on the 8th December and were given bivouac areas on the St Vith-Schonberg road. The Commanders were told to report to General Jones at his HQ in St Vith. They were greeted and given their orders: the take over would be carried out during the night of 9/10 December in blackout conditions and in total silence, the 2nd Division could then slip away to its new position hopefully undetected. Lieutenant-Colonel T. Paine Kelly Jr of the 589th Field Artillery Battalion supporting the 422nd Regiment was told that he had the honour of being the first to take over and

An American unit passes through the much-vaunted Siegfried Line – a toe hold had been gained on German territory.

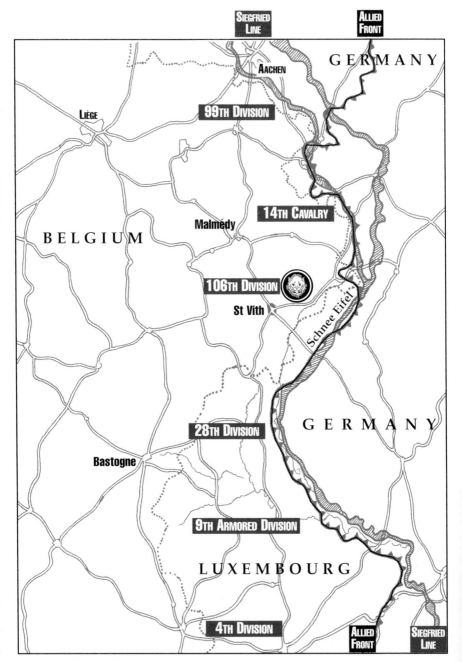

The Ghost Front

By December 1944 the Allies were up against the frontiers of Germany – the Siegfried Line defences had been penetrated at numerous points.

occupy its position. This was so it could register its fire in order that the other FAB's could comply accordingly. One firing battery section and his fire direction centre was to take over after 1600 on the 9th before it got too dark to achieve this. All Regimental and Battalion commanders were to reconnoitre their positions before dark and then meet their counterparts from the 2nd Division for briefing. The following morning Lieutenant-Colonel Kelly found his opposite number's Command Post in the kitchen of a German house along the Bleialf-Auw road. Its commander was pre-occupied with his own withdrawal. Unable to meet him, Kelly found the Executive Officer, a well-seasoned, experienced major in the HQ mess, situated in a patch of woods adjacent to the C.P. Coffee was poured, and the briefing completed, then the major told Kelly about the fears they had.

**Lieutenant-Colonel
T Paine Kelly, Jr**

The Divisional front was over-extended. If the Germans decided to attack from the east it was wide open; the Losheim Gap was only defended by a cavalry unit. The infantry was to the south and west of the batteries (See map of positions), and could not be expected to defend the artillery in the event of an attack. Not unduly worried about these reports Kelly started briefing his own staff. After all, he had been told on the way down from France that the Germans were virtually finished and this was a quiet front. His officers were shown on a map where and how to get to their assigned positions. At 11.30 the following morning the first salvo of 105mm shells barked away towards the German lines and the 589th Field Artillery Battalion was at war.

J. Don Holtzmuller was a Corporal Gunner of the number one howitzer of Battery A. He recalls:

'On 9th December we moved into the line about 1.5 miles south of Auw, Germany. We replaced a battery of the 2nd Infantry Division, gun for gun, as the 106th was relieving this division in the line. We were later told that when we had registered our gun (this is when the guns were aligned and coordinated for battle) our gun had fired the first round for

37

The 4th Section, Battery A, 589th Field Artillery Battalion. It was the 1st Section of this battery that fired the opening round of the war for the 106th Division on 9 December with a registration shot.

our division. The days between December 10th and the 15th were spent in getting used to living in the field and firing missions at targets in Germany. The men we relieved had built a hut, so we didn't have to live in tents. Everything was peaceful. We were told that this was a quiet sector and that we were just to get used to combat. We fired a lot of harassing missions at night, mostly aimed at sounds heard by our forward observers. The weather during this period was cloudy, with fog lasting for most of the daylight hours. We saw a lot of German V1 rockets, (more commonly known as Buzz Bombs) fly over our position. We were positioned under the path of their targets in Liège, Belgium and the English mainland.'

The rest of the Division had completed its relief by the 11th apart from the 424th Regt which got in the following day. On 11 December at 1900hrs the 106th Infantry Division officially assumed responsibility for that sector.

During quiet periods Lieutenant-Colonel Kelly went up to see his Regimental Commander, Colonel Descheneaux at his HQ. On one such occasion he brought up the subject of the Losheim Gap being open, and how so much depended on the group of cavalrymen from the 14th Cavalry in armoured cars and light Stuart tanks. Descheneaux just shrugged his shoulders saying, 'They won't let us do anything about it, the Roer Dam operation [an offensive to capture

Colonel Descheneaux

the dams of the Roer River, north of the 106th's positions] has not jumped off and HQ VIII Corps insist that there will be no change in disposition of forces.'

As Lieutenant-Colonel Thomas J. Riggs Jr of the 81st Combat Engineers remembers, 'The relief of the 2nd was accomplished in three days, man-for-man, and position-by-position'. As the 81st relieved the 2nd Engineer Combat Battalion, there was a lot of banter from these combat veterans about the 'country club' atmosphere of the position due to the daily exchange of fire but no real action. Lieutenant-Colonel Riggs went on to say,

'We inherited the fortifications, mine fields, and barbed wire which had been originally established by the 4th Infantry Division [back in September] *and reinforced by the 2nd "The new boys" also inherited the basic problem of these defensive positions.'*

But the men in the firing line didn't know that. They would find out only when it was too late.

So the 422nd and 423rd Regiments of the 106th went into the line, along with their accompanying units. With the 422nd Regiment went the 589th Field Artillery Battalion and with the 423rd went the 590th FAB. Each of the Artillery Battalions was equipped with twelve 105mm howitzers split into three batteries, with a Service Battery for each as back up behind the front. Also part of the Division was the 592nd FAB which served both Regiments with its 155mm howitzers. The other Regiment the 424th, was positioned a little further south of the Schnee Eifel and does not feature in this particular guide, (although I hasten to add, does not mean any disrespect to its members). Most of its action was fought separately around St Vith under the command of General Bruce Clarke's, US 7th Armored Division

The 2nd Division had been in these quiet positions for some time and had made themselves fairly comfortable. But they were now in a rush to move out, because of a coming attack towards the Roer River dams further north. Whilst speedily moving out they grabbed some of the new equipment the 106th had brought with them saying, 'You won't be needing that here. We'll leave you our old gear'. The turn over by officers was short and sweet and most of it shouted over their shoulders while leaving. For instance Colonel Boos of the 38th Infantry Regiment 2nd Division left Colonel Cavender of the 423rd standing by the side of the Bleialf-Schonberg road after saying, 'It has been quiet up here and your men will learn the easy way'. If only Colonel Boos had been right!

Into their positions the wet, cold and miserable men went. The 422nd and 423rd were actually in old German positions which were, of course, known to the enemy. The relief was completed by 11 December in thick snow and fog. In all the

A German bunker in the Siegfried Line defence system. These made excellent shelters for the GIs holding the line, but their exact postion was known to the enemy and were targeted with some accuracy during the coming German offensive.

Part of the Siegfried Line where the coming attack would break.

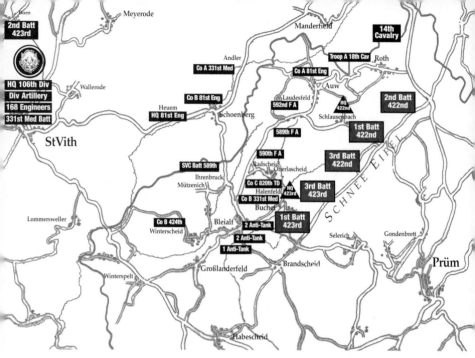

Disposition of main units on the Schnee Eifel and rear areas.

Division was extended some twenty-two miles; far too much for an infantry division. Normally a divisional front facing the Germans should have been at the most five miles. It was a dangerous scenario, but because it was supposed to be so quiet, VIII Corps overlooked the fact, saying this would not be a problem. Major General Jones and his Headquarters staff were ensconced in the old Sankt Josef's school in St Vith. The 81st Engineers were at the village of Heuem, approximately two miles west of Schonberg on the road that leads to St Vith. These combat engineers were split up so as to be able to help the infantry regiments by improving roads and general maintenance. Company A based at Auw aided the 422nd, and Company B at Schoenberg was with the 423rd. All these Engineers were commanded by Lieutenant-Colonel Thomas J Riggs. Also, medics of the 331st Medical Battalion had their HQ and clearing station at St Vith and the collecting companies disposed at Andler and Buchet. (These

Lieutenant-Colonel Thomas J Riggs

42

collecting stations are still there, as are most of the buildings mentioned in this guide).

The 422nd occupied the left hand side of the Schnee Eifel and had all three of its Battalions in the line. In command of that Regiment was Colonel George Descheneaux (whose headquarters was in the village of Schlausenbach, to the north). Covering seven miles of what was called the Losheim Gap, between the 106th and its nearest neighbour the 99th Division, was Colonel Mark Devine's 14th Cavalry. It covered the area the best it could. The 423rd on the right under Colonel Charles C Cavender had Buchet as their HQ. Its 2nd Battalion was in reserve at Born just north of St Vith and the 1st and 3rd Battalions were in the line on the right of the 422nd occupying the old Siegfried positions. From here the front line curved to the rear towards the village of Bleialf across open ground. To defend this exposed three mile gap between itself and the 424th Regiment, a Provisional Battalion from the 423rd was formed, consisting of its Anti Tank Company, part of its Cannon Company, one rifle

Headquarters of 422nd Infantry Regiment at Schlausenbach

Repairing a log cabin among the pine trees, on or near the German border, in the winter of 1944. Men, seasoned troops, of the Division that 106th replaced in the line, (2nd Division), had taken the stoves and fireplaces with them when they moved out.

platoon from the 3rd Battalion and C Company 820th Tank Destroyer Battalion dug in around Bleialf. Then, extending the line to the 424th Regiment, was B Troop 18th Cavalry Reconnaissance Squadron. Defence in depth had been sacrificed in order that the extended line could be covered. That was the defensive structure in the second week of December 1944.

After the initial shock of moving into the line the 106th found their new homes not so bad. Apart from the men up front stuck in foxholes, the rest were billeted in old Siegfried Line bunkers or timber-roofed dugouts. Although cold, at least it was shelter from the appalling weather. The 2nd Division had looted fires and stoves from the houses in the villages behind the line and made themselves really comfortable, but of course, being seasoned troops, had taken them with them. Again, as always in its short history, the men of the 106th Division were unlucky.

Gaining experience was top priority; patrolling with

maximum numbers was started. At first men were over-cautious, but that was to be expected. The rest of the troops settled down to the normal chores of front line soldiers.

The Tactical Problem

General Jones, the 106th Commander, sporting a dashing Don Ameche moustache, but who had never fired a shot in anger in nearly three decades as a soldier, was not happy with the positions the Division had inherited. He thought the road network was awful, especially in the area of the 422nd/423rd covered by this guide. On looking at the map, one can see that all the roads in the area lead to St Vith eventually and then fan out to all points of Belgium. In this area there are two roads from north to south, one from the Manderfeld direction that passes through Andler, Schonberg, Heuem and on to St Vith; the other from Auw down through Radscheid to Bleialf then either north to Schonberg or south west into the 424th area. The latter road was nicknamed 'Skyline Drive' or 'Skyline Boulevard' by the GIs as quite a bit of it was under observation from the German side. One part in particular, the corner just north of Bleialf where the Schonberg road meets the Skyline Drive was nicknamed 'Purple Heart' corner because anything that showed up there was bound to draw attention from the German guns in Brandscheid. Because of this the Engineers had built a corduroy road (log road, with tree trunks cut from the local forest) up through the woods from a spot on the Schonberg road and came out on the Skyline Drive near Radscheid. This effectively bypassed the dreaded corner, and was called 'Engineers Cut-Off'. There were also two roads that led out of Germany, one either side of the Schnee Eifel that ran into the two north-south roads.

Major General Alan W Jones

Jones surmised that if the Germans attacked down these two roads, not only would it cut his Division in half but, more dangerously, actually allow the enemy to surround the

Bend in the Schonberg road where the engineers constructed a corduroy road to avoid observation and fire from the German guns in Brandscheid. This became known as 'Engineers Cut-Off' and the route still exists coming out on the road once known as 'Skyline Drive' to Radscheid.

two Regiments on the hills. He and his staff were told not to worry, the Germans opposite were light, and also inexperienced, although there was a panzer division lurking somewhere behind, but that was a long way away and was probably in the throes of rebuilding after its mauling in France.

Even with this information and reassurance Jones decided to make some contingency plans and asked his Regimental Commanders to submit counter-attack and withdrawal ideas to headquarters. They never reached him in time.

The men began to improve their positions as best they could. The artillerymen obtained much-needed ammunition for their howitzers and adjusted the pits to give better registration of fire and started firing harassing rounds towards the German lines and also on target areas called for by the nervous riflemen up front. The latter were always imagining Germans lurking to their front. As one knows, if you stare long enough at an object like a tree trunk in the dark it starts to take on all sorts of guises and makes the mind race. The men were very jittery. The riflemen could do nothing to improve the poor fields of fire that lay in front of them. Most of them could see nothing but a sea of dense pine trees. From the top of the Schnee Eifel where the Battalion command posts were housed in the old Siegfried Line bunkers, towns could be observed through the murky fog to the east, but only if they were lucky. To cover the gap between the two regiments and to maintain contact with units either side, patrols were run at regular intervals.

Communications between units was by means of wire lines; in most cases this was only single cable, something else that had been inherited from the takeover. The 2nd Division had 'obtained' sound powered telephones which they utilized well, but of course they had taken those with them. Radios had been drawn in England but ever since the Division had left they had been under strict radio silence and this also applied to their present positions. Calibration and testing of the equipment had therefore been impossible.

Unfortunately, apart from Colonel Cavender and Brigadier General Perrin, no one else in the Divisional

A machine-gun position and guard post of the 589th Field Artillery Battalion in the Schnee Eifel.

command structure had ever seen any real action, and that had been 27 years before in the Great War. As a result the green troops had no one to turn to for reassurance. It was a worrying time for the inexperienced men of the 106th. Trench

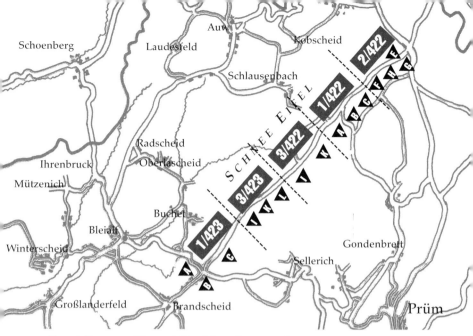

Front line position of the Line Companies

foot cases soared, especially in the 422nd Regt. No one had found time to dry out properly, and barrack bags with dry clothing had only just caught up with them. The issue of overshoes had taken far too long. Now on 14 December strange noises were heard to their front, engine noises! Once again they were told not to worry. A patrol was captured and the German officer in charge was found to have a copy of an attack order on him. This was rushed to the rear and never heard of again. A Polish deserter caught by a patrol from the 422nd spoke of a coming offensive. Another Pole who had stepped on a mine while trying to desert to the Americans turned up at one of the 331st Medical's clearing stations in Andler. Sergeant Thorpe was there, the man was badly hurt but was coherent and ready to talk, an American soldier was found who could speak his language. What he said amazed everybody. He had been pressed into the 12th SS and that unit had been moved up into forests, just east of the front line, under strict secrecy and would attack at night using searchlights, he was not sure quite when. Sergeant Thorpe remembers the young Intelligence officer hanging onto his every word, then scrambling for his jeep and heading off towards St Vith. Still nothing was done. German activity could be seen by the 423rd increasing in the area of Brandscheid. Company A's kitchen burned mysteriously and an abandoned building in the area caught fire, strangely drawing no fire. The sound of German patrols deep in the forest could be heard. Then on the night of the 15th an unidentified airplane flew low up and down the line drowning out strange, worrying noises. General Jones reported these facts to VIII Corps but in return was told, 'Don't be so jumpy, the Krauts are just playing phonograph records to scare you newcomers'.

Tension mounted by the hour. Something was going on. All the indications were there, but if the Intelligence men back at Division and Corps said there was no need for concern, then surely they must be right. The front settled down for another cold, wet, bonechilling night far from home. For many in the doomed 106th it was going to be the last night they would spend at peace!

Keeping watch on the Siegfried Line. A few miles to the front German units were moving up prior to their onslaught in the Ardennes. It was here that the brand new, untried, recently arrived 106th would take the full weight of Hitler's panzer grenadiers.

CHAPTER THREE

THE GERMAN PLAN
Operation 'Watch on the Rhine'

We have to go back to Saturday, 16 September, 1944. After his usual briefing held at his hidden field headquarters nicknamed the 'Wolf's Lair' in East Prussia, Hitler announced to his most trusted military staff, Field Marshal Wilhelm Keitel, Supreme Commander of the German Army, Alfred Jodl, Chief of Operations, Heinz Guderian, Commander of the Eastern Front and finally General Kreipe who represented an absent Air Marshal Göring that he was going over to the offensive. His plan was to counter-attack out of the Ardennes with Antwerp as the main objective. The small group of officers sat in silence; they could not believe

Hitler explains one of his plans to a group of dispirited officers in 1944.

their ears. Had the wounds received from the failed assination plot of July, when a bomb planted in a conference room exploded, finally taken their toll, along with the constant bad news from all fronts that the Germans were in full retreat?

The Führer did not appear to notice. He laid out his plans and ideas. As the Anglo-American armies had now stalled up against the vaunted 'Westwall', and the long supply columns were over-stretched to the extent that sufficient supplies were not reaching the front-line units, Hitler surmised that the Allied onslaught had petered out for the time being. He knew that the coalition between the Allies was rocky to say the least. He felt, too, that relationships between Russia and Britain were not of the best. If he could split the two armies in half, perhaps even surrounding one of them and take their key port away, the two Allied governments would fall out. Whilst this was going on he would be able to sue for peace under his terms, then turn his full attention to the main enemy, the Russians on the eastern front.

On 25 September Hitler told Jodl to start planning the new offensive. Keitel was given the job of sorting out how much fuel and ammunition would be needed and when it could be expected to be ready. Hitler himself formed a new army, the Sixth Panzer, which he gave command to a great favourite of his and former friend from the beer hall fighting days, General Josef 'Sepp' Dietrich. Its armoured divisions were all to be made up of Waffen SS.

German industry was at an all-time high, even though the Allies were constantly bombing. Manpower for the newly formed Volksgrenadier Divisions was achieved by enlisting naval and airforce personnel who had no ships or aircraft left, into the infantry. The call up ages

SS Colonel General 'Sepp' Dietrich

were changed so now boys of sixteen and men up to sixty were expected to join these Volksgrenadier (People's) divisions. The Area from Monschau in the north down to Echternach in the south was chosen for the breakthrough. This was because it was known by German intelligence that – as we have already seen – the American line here was the weakest and most overstretched. Terrain was poor and above all there were abundant forests on the German side of the Ardennes to conceal the attacking forces during the build-up. Weather as well was an important deciding factor,

Hitler, Keitel and Jodl. The Führer would come up with the idea and then the other two would put together the details.

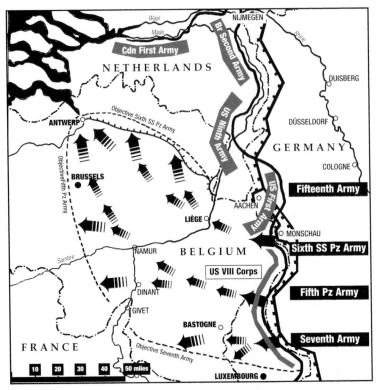

The German plan

the poorer the better as this would keep the Allied airforce grounded.

On 11 October Jodl met Hitler and gave him a rough plan, he called it by the operations name 'Christrose'. Three armies were to be used, the Fifth Panzer Army, the Sixth Panzer Army and the Seventh Army. These totalled twelve panzer and eighteen infantry divisions. Complete secrecy and bad weather was to play an important part; the Allied airforce must be grounded. The Armies would advance on a broad front, crossing the River Meuse by the second day and reaching Antwerp after one week. Thereupon the first of the 'red herring' messages was sent, announcing to all commanders of the Western Front that an offensive in that area was impossible but that a build-up of troops was necessary to block the Allied advance into Germany itself. Again the Western Allies were lulled into a false sense of security.

October 21 and Jodl met Hitler again, this time with the

last and final plan, Hitler was ecstatic about it and then, as another cover, gave it his own created codename 'Watch on the Rhine', a name, should the Allies hear of it, would only suggest a defensive build up. That same day Hitler entertained a certain Major Otto Skorzeny who had led the equivalent to the Allied commandoes on two daring raids: one to rescue Mussolini from certain capture by the Allies and the other and more recent, to grab the head of the Hungarian Government before it surrendered. Hitler congratulated Skorzeny on his deeds and then informed him of a greater mission. He was to select and train a unit that would be able to dress and talk like Americans, travel in US vehicles and create as much havoc and confusion as possible behind the American lines. He was to capture key bridges and hold certain areas until the advancing armies could reach him. A tall order indeed but one that was very much suited to Skorzeny. At the same time Hitler promoted him to Colonel.

Major Otto Skorzeny would train and lead a commando team with orders to cause disruption behind American lines.

The following day Hitler sent plans to Field Marshal Gerd von Rundstedt, who was then Commander in Chief of the Western Front, and to Field Marshal Walther Model whom Hitler personally had selected as commander of the entire offensive. Both on seeing the plan thought it ludicrous. Model commented 'This damned thing hasn't a leg to stand on'. The two men then went on to configure their own plans. Rundstedt's was called 'Martin' and Model's 'Autumn Fog'. When presented to Hitler, he threw them out saying that they

Field Marshal
Walther Model

When the German Commander in Chief in the West, Field Marshal Gerd von Rundstedt, saw Hitler's plan for attacking in the Ardennes he immediately began drawing up his own – as did Field Marshal Model. Both were rejected by the Führer who considered his own more daring.

should follow his example in copying Frederick the Great, who had defeated enemies of much greater strength by taking a big risk.

After all the different plans and ideas had been presented to him, by 7 December Hitler had made up his own mind and could not be swayed. His original plan was the one to be used.

In the planning, security was very tight, apart from the need to leak messages to the enemy. Everything covering the offensive was entrusted to 'officer hand mail' only, and they themselves were sworn to secrecy under threat to their own lives or their families. Briefing began of the corps commanders but only on 'the need to know basis'. 'Buzzes' were spread around soldiers' haunts that they were only in the front line for defensive reasons, in case some might defect or there were spies about.

At the same time all tracks pointed west. The railroads worked flat out and only at night, carrying troops and supplies to pre-designated railheads just east of the Ardennes. Radio communications ceased. Germany went silent and only transmitted messages the military wanted the Allies to hear, 'Nothing happening, all build-ups for defensive purposes only,' Allied Intelligence at the top reported.

The final briefings took place: Sixth Panzer Army under Dietrich to attack through the Ardennes between Monschau and the Losheim Gap, cross the River Meuse and head for Antwerp; the Fifth Panzer army commanded by General Hasso von Manteuffel was to surround the Schnee Eifel cutting off the US 106th Division and then capture the all-important road hub of St Vith, whilst the remainder of his army would attack through Luxembourg, wheel north, cross the Meuse, through Brussels and on to Antwerp, protecting the flank of the Sixth Army. The Seventh Army under General Erich Brandenberger, to the south of the other two had the job of protecting Manteuffel's southern flank against possible threats from Patton's Third Army.

The date was set for 16 December, 1944, H Hour 0530. The 106th waited.

On 13 December the last of the reports came into Hitler's Headquarters: reports consisting of details of manpower, fuel storage and amounts and quantities of ammunitions. Each tank had enough fuel to

General Hasso von Manteuffel Fifth Panzer Army

General Erich Brandenburger Seventh Army

Build up of German troops behind the Schnee Eifel was hidden from the eyes of the Allies, who preferred to believe that there was no danger of attack in this sector.

Panthers and their crews who would be used in the coming offensive.

General Hasso von Manteuffel consults with junior officers prior to the attack.

take it approximately 90 miles, each gun 60 rounds, etc etc. The following night the armies moved their attacking forces up to within 3 miles of the front line, German aircraft flew up and down the lines to blot out the noise of this taking place, also straw was spread thickly on the roads to muffle the sound. These were the strange noises that the men in their foxholes on the Schnee Eifel could hear, but were told not to worry about. Worry they might. Just in front of them shielded by the thick forests were some 300,000 men, 1,900 guns and 970 tanks and assault guns waiting for the signal to attack through the 85-mile Ardennes front.

The following is a selection of captured documents used to address the German troops prior to the attack.

> *Soldiers of the West Front! Your great hour has arrived. Large attacking armies have started against the Anglo-Americans. I do not have to tell you anything more on that. You feel it yourself:*
> *WE GAMBLE EVERYTHING!*
> *You carry with you the holy obligation to give everything to achieve things beyond human possibilities for Our Fatherland and our Führer!*
>
> VON RUNDSTEDT
> C in C West
> Generalfeldmarschall

Addition to the order of the day of C in C West. We will not disappoint the Führer and the Homeland who created the sword of revenge. Advance in the spirit of Luther. Our password will remain now more than ever: No soldier of the world can be better than we soldiers of the Eifel and Aachen area.

MODEL
Generalfeldmarschall
Dist: Feldjäger Kdo z.B.V., G-3
66 Corps G-3, Chief of Section

Forward double time! Remember the heritage of our dead comrades as well as the tradition of our proud Wehrmacht.

VON MANTEUFFEL
General d. Panzertruppen
Dist: Feldjäger Kmdo z.B.V., G-3
66 Corps G-3, Chief of Section.

It seems strange that the Allied command did not heed the warning signs, or, did they just want to get the Germans out into the open once and for all? It is not for this book to go into deep aspects of it, but to provide an insight and guide. Only one man in Allied Intelligence was fairly certain of what was going on. He was Colonel Benjamin A. 'Monk' Dickson, top man of First Army Intelligence. He had read through some of the reports that were now filtering in from the front and surmised that something was wrong. He was convinced that the Germans were going to attack and even named the Ardennes. But the powers that be thought Dickson had been overworking and was getting nervous over nothing. He was sent to Paris on 15th December for a much needed rest. The last opportunity to do something was lost.

Chapter Four

THE ATTACK

Saturday, 16th December 1944

Saturday 16 December at 0530 the German barrage began. Darkness and fitful slumber were still among the young men of the Golden Lions; it was the rudest awakening anyone had ever experienced. Guns of every calibre fired their might on to pre-designated targets up and down the line. Huge 14 inch guns even hit St Vith miles behind the front. Not only had the Germans been watching and noting American key positions but also had actually penetrated with reconnaissance patrols through the gaping holes in the lines to gain vital information. With this intelligence and the fact that they knew the land so well, (after all they had been in the same positions only a few months before) the German gunners were able to hit American targets with uncanny accuracy.

As the attack began the German gunners were able to hit American targets with uncanny accuracy.

Communication land lines were soon knocked out. With absolutely no idea what was going on to the left and right of them, groups of riflemen began to think that the barrage was intended solely for them. Scattered hazy reports began to infiltrate back to divisional headquarters. Men rushed from their warm beds and manned their positions. Gripping their rifles, scared and shocked they stared to their front.

At the school house in St Vith General Jones sifted through the sketchy messages trying to piece together what was happening. VIII Corps had been alerted but was convinced that it was no more than a spoiling attack, but to keep them informed. General Jones was quoted as saying 'When they drop 14 inch shells on you it's the real thing'. The messages began to pour in, 0550 am from the 423rd, relayed over the artillery circuit: '423 Inf AT Co shelled by arty since 5:30. 2nd Bn 423 Inf alerted. Lines out with AT Co, 2nd Bn and Tr B, 14 Cav Gr'. With these kind of messages buzzing through the airways Jones began to suspect this was no spoiling attack.

By 0615 the barrage had stopped, flares soared into the air and in certain open places, like crossroads, strange eerie lights appeared. These were huge searchlight beams bouncing off the low thick clouds in order to illuminate areas

Volksgrenadiers moving up during the attack.

The 18th VGD had only been recently formed in Denmark from Luftwaffe and navy personnel.

artificially as if by moonlight.

The men began to see figures, waves of shadows, some dressed in snow suits leaping through the trees to their front, and now could be heard the noise of vehicles and the clanking of tracks. These figures were the German soldiers of Generalmajor Gunther Hoffman-Schonborn's 18th Volks-grenadier Division (VGD) and Oberst Friedrich Kittel's 62nd VGD. The 18th VGD was made up of three regiments, the 293rd, 294th and the 295th. It was formed in late summer 1944 in Denmark, and was made up of many Luftwaffe and Kriegsmarine personnel. By November it had a complement of nigh on 10,000 officers and men, and was training in the Ardennes region. To aid the attack, Hetzers and Sturmgeschütz self-propelled assault guns were attached to the grenadiers. The mission of the 18th VGD was to encircle the Schnee Eifel, close behind the 106th Division at Schonberg and move on to take the important road and rail hub of St Vith. The 62nd VGD was slightly to the south and was to attack between the 424th and 423rd regiments, generally heading north-west, also towards St Vith.

The sole purpose of these two divisions was to open up the road network in the centre of the Ardennes to allow support for the major thrusts west of the Sixth Panzer Army in the north and the Fifth Panzer Army in the south. The timetable they were given was of the gravest importance and stipulated St Vith must be captured by the evening of the 17th or, at the latest, early in the morning of 18 December.

In the Eifel, Hoffman-Schonborn opted to send one regiment around the north, one round the south and to keep his third regiment immediately in front of the 106th positions.

The 'spooky', strange happenings of the past weeks were over, the figures coming at the 106th through the German positions were at long last something the Americans could understand.

Sitting in a makeshift log lean-to, built by Engineers, alongside one of the bunkers which had been bulldozed, was Acting NCO Anthony J. Marino of HQ Company 1st Battalion 422 Infantry:

Anthony J. Marino

'I was in the Command post seated at the telephone table with the log sheets of the companies in deployment. When, crack - crack, two 88mm bursts pierced the darkness, one falling short – one hitting the upper part of the wall where a Lieutenant and a Sergeant were seated. Colonel Kent [Commander of the 1st Battalion] *was standing talking in front of the table at which I was seated. Colonel Kent was 6 feet 2 tall. The second 88 burst hit the upper portion of the wall splintering the logs and crashing them across the upper room – Colonel Kent was caught in the burst. He did not have his helmet on. The damage was fatal, splinters entering his neck and the back of his head. Medics attended to him. However, the fatal 16th of December made it impossible for him to be evacuated to an army field hospital where he could have been treated competently. There was this gaping hole in the wall, Colonel Kent was thrown*

across the table I was seated at. The Lieutenant was hit with a piece of log which caused a severe bump on his back. I scurried in haste – filled with anxiety. Sergeant Kerski came into the command post saying, "There are Germans all through the area"! I yelled, "The fire, the fire put out the fire in the fire place". I ran and dumped the large coffee pot on to the smouldering fire. It. went out. I said, "We have got to get out of here – we will be easy prey to anyone coming in". We mutually went for the door. Outside in the subzero temperature there was calm.'

Up to the north the Germans swept through their pre-designated channel like muck through a goose. The 14th Cavalry defending the gap between the 106th and the 99th Division fell back in disarray; not their fault, as like everyone else they had only inherited positions that others had established. Normally a cavalry unit was used for screening and reconnaisance, not to dismount from their armoured cars and light tanks to defend static areas.

The German southerly regiment, the 293rd of the 18th VGD, came spilling out of the village of Brandscheid and up the road from Prum. Their first target was the small town of Bleialf. The right flank of the 423rd regiment poured everything they had onto the massed German attack. The 1st Battalion in and around the Schnee Eifel stood firm but the makeshift forces covering the open ground began to give a little.

Volksgrenadiers came flooding up the railway cutting just south west of Bleialf, effectively driving a wedge between the 423rd and the 424th Regiments, completely cutting off Troop B 18th Cavalry Squadron. Vast numbers of German troops attacked out of the woods and were soon in and around the town. Bleialf was now virtually in enemy hands with all communications lost. Realizing what was going on, Cavender mustered his only reserve force, a Service Company based at Halenfeld. At 0905 he managed to get a message through to HQ at St Vith telling them that Troop B was in trouble and needed help and that he was committing

Colonel Charles Cavender

his reserve. He also requested that he should be given B Company 81st Engineers based at Schonberg, which was approved.

The Engineers moved out and detrucked on the outskirts of Bleialf. They went into action straight away as riflemen; the remnants of Cannon Company and the other units which formed Captain Charles B Reid's Composite Battalion also joined in the effort to retake the town.

With fire support from Company C 820th Tank Destroyer Battalion and the 590th FAB, the mixed group fought their way through the town in vicious house to house fighting, Cavender sent every available man he had, even his headquarters staff. Bleialf must be retaken to re-establish the southern link.

Bodies now littered the streets, much of the fighting was hand-to-hand. (Two days later when the town's priest ventured out of his cellar, he found in excess of 200 bodies, both German and American, in the vicinity of his church.) By 1500 the makeshift American force managed to clear the place of Germans and retake the town except for the few houses leading to the railway station. By noon Lieutenant-

There was heavy fighting for the German village of Bleialf – much of it hand to hand – as 81st Combat Engineers fought as infantry. Here a GI loads his Garand M1 with new clip. Around him are German dead.

Colonel Frederick W. Nagle, the Regimental Executive, was sent there to take charge.

John Hillard Dunn was now a Combat MP (Military Policeman) guarding about fifty German prisoners. Towards evening wounded began to filter into his positions. He had a chance to talk to a man from Cannon Company. His was the story of a forlorn, desperate little action in the German town of Bleialf: 'So you wanta know what the hell Cannon Company is doing – fighting in Bleifel,' he said as he rubbed the bandage on his right leg. 'The god-damned Heinie infantry takes Bleialf in a surprise move. Our rifle companies are too damned busy to do anything about it. Besides, Cannon's run out of ammunition for the guns by now anyway.'

He stopped to light a cigarette.

'Understand, I ain't beefin', but hell, village fighting with carbines and damned few grenades ain't no picnic. What the hell, though, somebody's got to try to take the damned town back. Ain't no other way of getting to division at St.Vith.'

This made Dunn realize the reason why he had been unable to get his prisoners back to Division. They were cut off.

'We take her back,' the GI went on to tell Dunn. 'Don't ask me how. They don't let us keep it long. They come back with artillery fire, and then mortars and then infantry. There's Cannon guys left back there but they ain't movin'.'

He lit another cigarette from his butt. 'That's how it is, Mac. But where the hell do we go from here?'

Whilst all this fighting was going on, the 3rd Battalion 423rd up in the Schnee Eifel sat totally untouched save for a few skirmishes with German patrols. They were, however, helping their neighbours the 1st Battalion by concentrating fire down on to the Sellerich road.

John Kline was a nineteen-year-old heavy machine-gun squad leader, with the rank of Sergeant:

'I was with M Company 423rd Combat Infantry Regiment, Third Battalion. I was not aware that the Battle of the Bulge, as it later became known, had started. My impression was that Bleialf was to my right rear. My gun

John Kline

position on the Eifel was on the extreme left flank of the 423rd Regiment. In fact there was only one rifleman to my left. There were patrols that passed back and forth through the unprotected area between the 423rd and the 422nd Regiment. My Commander's command post was in one of the old fortresses, which was located back of me and to the right. From the CP I could see Buchet and some of the valley in between that city and our positions. From my dugout position, on the German side of the Eifel, all I could see was a forest of trees. I think this was the reason we were not aware of the fierce fighting going on at Bleialf. I had a 300-400 yard cleared area in front of my dugout and there was very little daylight that showed through. We had to cross an open field back of us to get to the CP and the mess tent. This on occasion would draw some German artillery'.

The 2nd Battalion, 423rd had been in reserve north of St Vith in the town of Born, but by that afternoon had been alerted by Headquarters and told to move out by truck to Schonberg. Once there they were to dig in and defend the town from possible threat from the south and northeast. By 1730 they were in position. Lieutenant-Colonel Joseph P. Puett, commanding the 2nd Battalion, immediately sent out patrols to see what was going on and by 1930 sent a clear

Moving up over difficult terrain.

message to St Vith:

'Enemy shelling Schonberg heavily. Cavalry have withdrawn and are mining the road five hundred yards north of Andler. Enemy have completely taken Auw. The 275th Armored Field Artillery have also withdrawn. [This was a 105mm self propelled unit attached to the 14th Cavalry]. *Am patrolling in three directions and will have more information at 2000'.*

With the 2nd Battalion was Charles Paetschke. He had only been in the Division a short while, transferring from the 104th Division shortly before the 106th shipped out from the States. He and a couple of other GIs had been given some dummy bazooka rounds to fire at a target. To his elation he had scored a direct hit. When it came to a live firing he narrowly missed, but all the same, he was made a bazookaman. Which he now regretted. In Born he was billeted in a school house. Down the road was a bar of a fashion, more like someone's front room, where they would all sit around a large table buying beers with their occupation currency. Moving by transport to Schonberg, Charles found a large empty building and along with numerous other soldiers tried to bed down for the night.

Communications began to get back in, wiremen from the signal detachments went out in search of broken lines. Joseph Remetta was a lineman in the 106th Signal Company:

'In the Ardennes, the Signal Company had the Division forward switchboard in Schonberg, and there were four of us trouble shooters staying in the same house as the switchboard. On the first day of the Bulge all the lines went out early to the regiments. Sergeant Davis and myself went to the 422nd and the 423rd, while the other two trouble shooters went to the 424th. After a while we spotted a break in a cable on some open ground. We would be exposed to enemy fire if we went to fix it, but the wiremen from the regiment and myself decided that we would run to the break, hit the dirt, and do what we had to do, then get out of there. While we were making the splice, our artillery from the rear was laying down some pretty heavy barrages. You could hear the shells passing overhead and landing in a wooded area

about 300 yards ahead. Also about 10 yards ahead of us, one of our machine-gunners was doing an awful lot of firing. Some of the infantry riflemen were behind us firing from behind a roll in the terrain. So I guess the Germans didn't have time to pay any attention to us.'

On their arrival back at the switchboard that evening they found the house had been damaged quite a bit, there were large hunks of shrapnel inside.

Meanwhile to the north that morning, the 422nd Regiment was having troubles of its own. The German Grenadiers had driven the 14th Cavalrymen out of the villages of Krewinkel, Roth and Kobscheid and were hammering on the door of Auw. This would jeopardize the entire left flank and also meant the gateway to the rear of the two American Regiments would be open. Company A of the 81st Engineers held this village. When they had been awoken that morning by the German barrage they were astonished to find the occupants of the village already dressed and sheltering in

A Panther clears the trees during the attack.

their cellars. The evening before a woman had been spotted going from house to house. Later they suspected she had informed the villagers of the German attack.

Approximately 15 to 20 rounds fell on the village four of which hit their command post, fortunately no one was hurt. The Engineers, not knowing any better, set to work just like any other day, repairing the damage to the roads. At about 0930 they were interrupted by small arms fire coming from the direction of Roth, the engineers immediately sought cover and returned fire. Lieutenant William J. Coughlin had taken his 1st Platoon to Schlausenbach that morning to work and on hearing the firing up at Auw had dashed back with his platoon to help. They made it back to their quarters and started taking on the Germans milling about on the edge of the village.

Roth had fallen to the Germans by midday and they were now concentrating on their next objective, Auw. The engineers were putting up a brave fight against incalculable odds, but when tanks appeared it was time to get out. Most made it back to Heuem via Andler but one group was trapped in a house with only an open field behind them. With the Germans advancing towards them there seemed no way but to stand and fight until overrun. Sergeant Withee offered to stay and hold off the enemy whilst the rest of his comrades made a run for it. He took on the Volksgrenadiers single-handed, it was not until the building was virtually blown away around him did he stop firing and finally surrendered. Later he had a rest centre at Eupen named after him in his honour and was awarded the Distinguished Service Cross.

Auw was in German hands, and they were now trying tentative thrusts further, towards Andler and up the road (Skyline Drive) that cuts through the artillery positions and leads to Bleialf.

All morning the 589th, 590th, and 592nd Field Artillery Battalions had been saving the day, supporting the infantry everywhere with well concentrated salvoes that crashed down on German formations. However, it soon became clear that the enemy was getting too close for comfort. Early in the

Manhandling a 57mm M1 field piece into position.

Artillery men of the 106th Infantry Division fusing shells during the battle.

afternoon armoured vehicles began to appear through the gloom on the road up from Auw. Lieutenant Eric Fisher Wood Jr, of Battery A, ran to a hillock to his left to get a better view and managed to get a howitzer onto them. Over open sights the cannon managed to send the leading assault gun up in a sheet of flames, causing the following vehicles and troops to withdraw to cover.

The artillery now began to organize a road block and local security to protect itself from the threats.

J. Don Holtzmuller:

'Our first day of real battle was very harrowing. Our gun was unable to fire on the tanks, which appeared in front of our position since a log fence had been built around our gun and one of the upright posts of the fence was right in line with the tank. Also, a German artillery shell had buried itself in the mud about 20 feet in front of our gun, but luckily it was a dud and didn't explode.'

Descheneaux, commander of the 422nd, realizing the danger, sent a mixed force of available men up from his HQ area in Schlausenbach to try and retake Auw and secure his left flank. As the men began crossing open ground in front of the village a snow blizzard and heavy enemy fire greeted them. They were forced to turn back and confirmed the news that the Germans definitely were at Auw and in some strength.

Divisional Headquarters now realized the danger that was unfolding all across their front, and decided to get the 589th and 592nd artillery withdrawn. Still Jones awaited some kind of message from his Corp Commander Major General Troy Middleton.

An order to move his Battalion up to the north was received by Puett at Schonberg, directing him to help the two field artillery battalions to displace and withdraw. He was also to protect the left flank of the 422nd Regiment.

The welcome news reached St Vith that the 9th Armored Division's Combat Command B was on its way to help. Immediately, Jones told them that they were to attack towards Schonberg the following day, and by doing so relieve the situation on the Schnee Eifel.

Back at Vielsalm, under orders from Headquarters the

106th Divisional Band broke up its rehearsals, swopped the musical instruments for weapons and headed for St Vith to become the headquarters guard.

Finally Jones got the call from Middleton. It was a guarded conversation as both commanders thought the line was being tapped. As a result of their clipped conversation both parties failed to understand what the other was saying. By the end of it Jones was convinced that he was supposed to keep his regiments in place, and further, that Middleton was sending the 7th Armored Division to help from its position up north; and that it was due to arrive the following morning. Armed with this mis-information Jones felt much better. He immediately called off previous plans for the 9th Armored and instead sent them south to support the 424th Regiment. When the 7th Armored arrived in St Vith the next day he would send it on to Schonberg. Colonel Slayden, an intelligence officer on loan to Jones from Corps, realized that this was an impossible task – he knew that the 7th could not possibly reach them by the next morning, it was over 60 miles away. After the war he admitted he should have said something to Jones, but at the time it would have sounded as though he was calling the Corps Commander a liar.

Meanwhile the 2nd Battalion, 423rd, at about 1930 drove from Schonberg south on the Bleialf road, up Engineers Cut-Off and along the Skyline Drive, finally reaching the artillery positions at about midnight. Charles Paetschke had not been

A Battery of 155mm Howitzers taking up a new position during the Battle.

asleep for very long before he heard shouts of 'move out'! He collected his gear together and went out into the street only to find the jeep with his bazooka in it had gone. He felt a great relief at his loss as he joined others clambering into the back of a truck for the journey up to Auw. Through sheer exhaustion he nodded off to sleep next to the tailgate. The first jolt of the truck sent his helmet flying out the back. What a way to be entering combat for the first time, he thought, no helmet and no bazooka.!

In the meantime, the artillerymen were preparing to get out. It was hard going trying to drag the howitzers out of their muddy emplacements and some had to be left. Finally the 6x6 prime movers got the rest of them going and they set off in the dark snowy night. New positions had been found for them, the 592nd was to go back to St Vith and the 589th to the vicinity of its service battery about three miles south of Schonberg.

J. Don Holtzmuller:

That night, as we were loading up to move back to a new position, machine-gun fire with tracers continually flew over our heads. We were on the edge of a wooded area and the Germans were firing just above the tops of the trees. The enemy must have mistaken the treetops for the ground.'

Whilst all this was going on, Descheneaux swung his left hand Battalion the 2nd, round to face north. So at the end of the first day the 106th had not given much ground. The 423rd Regiment had retaken Bleialf but had not gained contact

with its sister regiment to the south, and the 422nd Regiment still held the Schnee Eifel and had swung its left hand battalion around to guard the north and into which Puett's 2nd Battalion had joined and extended that line.

If the German timetable was to go according to plan Schonberg must be taken in the morning, so far the GIs of the 106th had denied them their prize.

Sunday 17th December 1944

Throughout the night of the 16/17 the Germans poured through the now wide open Losheim Gap, desperately trying to by-pass the stubborn resistance of the 106th on the Schnee Eifel. The 14th Cavalry had been pushed back and was still desperately trying to form a solid defence line. The road leading to St Vith was jammed with rear echelon traffic streaming west to get away from the front.

In his headquarters Jones received an order from the VIII Corps commander Middleton, dated 0036 17 December, 'Troops will be withdrawn from present position only if position becomes completely untenable'. Jones would have to sit tight. About an hour later contact was made with Brigadier General William M. Hoge of Combat Command B, 9th Armored Division. Thinking that the 7th Armored Division would be with them by 0700 Jones sent CCB down the road to help the 424th Regiment at Winterspelt. They would be moving into position at daybreak

The defenders of Bleialf got wind that something major was going to happen to them as early as 0255 when a German prisoner told them of the plan to retake the village. Colonel Cavender forwarded the news onto Division. GI patrols confirmed the threat when they observed Germans building up and preparing for the assault. Incoming artillery fire, of all calibres, was increasing. At 0600 the Germans rushed from the direction of the railway tunnel near the village and swept through the town forcing the defenders to scatter. Immediately the engineers were overrun. The remainder of the defenders made it back to Buchet and the comparative safety of the 423rd Regiment. It was a fighting withdrawal all the way.

With the stubborn defence broken, the German grenadiers of the 293rd Regiment pushed on up the road towards Radscheid and Schonberg. About an hour later the village of Andler, at the northern hinge of the German encirclement, also fell. The small group of men from the 32nd Cavalry Reconnaissance Squadron's Troop B, in their lightly armed armoured cars, had no chance of stopping the inrush of grenadiers. Some King Tiger tanks from the 506th Heavy Panzer Battalion, which had strayed into the fray by accident whilst looking for decent routes to their own objective, joined in the attack. Troop B withdrew, first to Schonberg where they found that Bleialf had fallen, then back to the village of Heuem. The Volksgrenadiers were close on their heels, but fortunately for the cavalrymen the Tigers had continued on in another direction.

GIs pour fire into the attacking Germans.

The 590th FAB, which had been pouring fire into Bleialf, realized it too was in danger of being overrun.

The 2nd Battalion, 423rd in the old 589th FAB positions sent out patrols which discovered an enemy build up of armour in Auw. At about 0700 three tanks started probing up the road towards their positions. Puett's 3-inch anti-tank guns made short work of them. However, the attackers were determined and more tanks rumbled into view, this time with infantry riding on the back of them. These were immediately engaged with the result that they were dispersed to cover. Relentlessly, the Germans began to advance again towards Puett's position. He had lost touch with the 422nd Regiment to his right, also wire communications with Division were out and then his radio was suddenly shot to pieces. There was nothing for it but to withdraw falling back to Schonberg. He sent out patrols to check out the route only to have them report back that 'Kraut armour was bumper to bumper on the Bleialf-

Men of the 106th during the fighting.

Schonberg road'. His retreat from encirclement was gone. An officer arrived from the 590th FAB and after some hurried consultation the decision was taken for both groups to fall back on to the positions of the 423rd Regiment on the Schnee Eifel. This they did, covering each other all the way. On arrival, Cavender had them slot into the perimeter defence which was already forming around the southern nose of the ridge. He also shifted his command post from Buchet to one of the bunkers in his 3rd Battalion area within the Siegfried Line. The time was about mid-morning.

Also Descheneaux, commanding the 422nd, realized that his rear was now in jeopardy, what with Puett's 2nd/423rd Battalion gone and with Germans beginning to feel their way down the Skyline Drive. He adjusted his regiment by taking some of the not as yet hard-hit men from his 3rd Battalion to bolster the fully involved 1st Battalion, which was also being called on to form a rear defensive position. The 2nd Battalion, which was facing north, had rushed into this position the previous evening having left its field kitchens, supplies and kitbags, and was now running short of food. Descheneaux decided to try and feed them from the kitchens of the other two battalions. At 09.30 he sent a message to Division with words to that effect, and added,

'Estimate sufficient rations to last today, no reserve on hand, out of communications with motor pool... Doubt their ability to leave bivouac. Almost complete unit load of ammunition on hand. Request immediate action to remedy above situation.'

Casualties for both regiments had been surprisingly light up until now. Because of the lack of communications, he had not received the message informing him that the 589th was to withdraw, and so thought he had just temporarily lost touch with them.

The 589th FAB had moved into their new positions at about 07.30. These were just beside the Schonberg-Bleialf road, about three miles south of Schonberg, almost on the Belgian-German border. No sooner had they dropped the guns' trails, than an urgent message was received from their Service Battery, a little more than a mile to the south, and still occupying their original positions. It reported being under attack from strong German armoured units. Then the lines went dead. Almost immediately a truck appeared coming up the road at speed. The driver brought his vehicle to a halt and, indicating back down the road, shouted that enemy tanks were not far behind him. Once again the men of the 589th set about hitching their howitzers up to the prime movers; this time they were to take them back to St Vith. Yet again the heavy pieces were getting bogged down in the freezing mud. A Battery got three of its howitzers out onto the road and set off through Schonberg and onto St Vith. The fourth piece was proving especially difficult to move, but the crew were determined not to leave it behind. B Battery was also experiencing problems and suddenly bullets began zipping through the air all around them. The pieces were ordered abandoned. The men pitched into their trucks and followed A Battery down the road in the direction of St Vith.

J. Don Holtzmuller, B Battery:

'No sooner had we made everything ready than someone came running down through the position yelling, "March Order! Get out of here, the Germans are coming!" A weapons carrier then pulled into the lane between where our truck had parked and the howitzer, the weapons carrier got stuck in the mud. We closed trails on the gun and were able to roll the gun out by hand. We were then able to push the weapons carrier out and finally we moved our truck down to the ammunition so that it could be reloaded onto the truck. We hooked up the gun to the truck and drove out to the road with the hope that we were on our way to safety in St Vith. The other three sections had driven off at the first shout.'

Major Elliot Goldstein, acting executive officer of the 589th managed, after much difficulty, to get a message by phone through to Division: 'Service Battery and one firing Battery overrun, unable to get howitzers into position. Tanks one mile from Schonberg coming up road from Bleialf.' The time was 0820.

J. Don Holtzmuller goes on to say,

'We had driven just a short distance down the road and started down the hill into the little village of Schonberg when

we suddenly saw a German armoured vehicle parked in the middle of the road. We subsequently found out that the machine we had thought was a tank was really a self-propelled gun. Our driver stopped at once. None of us fired our small arms, nor did the German fire at us as he was parked so that his gun was aimed down the hill and not directed towards our truck. The German then drove off down the hill and around a curve, where we lost sight of him. Immediately thereafter a jeep pulled up behind us and our Executive Officer, Lieutenant Eric Wood, jumped out and asked us why we had stopped. We told him we had just seen a German tank. He said "It couldn't be. It was probably an American tank". He climbed into the cab of our truck along with Corporal Knoll, our driver, and Sergeant Scannapico our section leader, and said "Let's go".

'So off we went, down the hill, around the curve and on toward a little stone bridge, which crossed the Our River into the middle of the little village. The Lieutenant then saw a tank parked to the side of a house and said, "See, it's an American tank". Then he looked again and said, 'Hell! no it isn't! It's a German! Pour on the gas". As we passed the tank the German fired at us and missed. Private Campagna, who was

Damaged Weapons Carrier belonging to 592nd Field Artillery Battalion. German horse drawn artillery unit on the road moving west. A dead American soldier lies in the foreground.

manning a bazooka, fired at the tank and also missed but he hit a house and blew a hole in the side of it. We then thought we were home free and on the road to St.Vith, but when we went around a curve we faced another self-propelled gun with its cannon pointed right at us. We also saw about three or four German soldiers with automatic weapons beside the gun. Corporal Knoll stopped the truck and we enlisted men jumped off to the left into a ditch. Lieutenant Wood jumped out the opposite side and ran up the hill into the woods. Immediately after we had got clear the German self-propelled gun fired a round into the motor of our truck, blowing metal and shrapnel all around. One American truck had been stopped before ours and when we escaped from the truck to the ditch, we found that we had joined a Lieutenant-Colonel and four black soldiers from an American 155-mm artillery battalion.

There were several of the these artillery battalions around this area, they were Corp units attached to the 106th Division. One of these was the 333rd Field Artillery Battalion dug-in in the Schonberg area, and manned by black soldiers. Beside the road between the villages of Herresbach and Wereth is a newly erected monument in memory of eleven of its members. These men were captured by an SS unit, clubbed, bayoneted and shot then left lying beside the road at this spot. The monument reads: 'Here on 12/17/44 eleven U.S Soldiers were shot by the SS. [12/17/44 = 17 December 1944.]

'After discussing the situation, and realizing that there was no cover to run to and that our few carbines would be almost useless against a bunch of automatic weapons, we decided that to do anything other than surrender would be automatic suicide. We walked out of the ditch with our hands in the air. Once out of the ditch, we found the truck driver, Corporal Knoll, lying in the road, shot through both ankles and also wounded with shrapnel from the artillery round. The Germans searched us, taking food, cigarettes, watches etc. They subsequently indicated we should start back up the road towards Germany.'

Quite a few other trucks began to pull up behind

SS Panzer grenadiers during the Battle of the Bulge. Atrocities committed by men of these units did much to stiffen the resolve of the Allied soldiers.

Holtzmuller's and the crews of these were also captured. Holtzmuller wanted to stay and help Corporal Knoll but the Germans had other ideas and forced him on. He subsequently found out later that Knoll was killed in action. Also, whilst walking back, he noticed Sergeant Scannapico's body lying by the side of the road. At what point the latter had left the truck he never found out, but he had probably left the cab to shoot at some infantry soldiers he had seen and was shot down.

Lieutenant Eric Fisher Wood was the only man to escape this debacle, he had out-run the German bullets and made it to the safety of the dark forest. On 18 December Peter Maraite, a local, was out getting a tree for Christmas when he came across Wood and another soldier and led them back to his house. There they were fed and allowed to stay for the night, despite the fact that the area was crawling with Germans. In statements given by the Maraite family, it appears that Lieutenant Wood had told them that if he was unable to get back to the American lines, he would remain in the area and conduct a war of his own. In the following days small arms fire was heard coming from the woods, and reports from wounded Germans coming back seemed to confirm that they were being ambushed on the rough forest tracks. These were being used by the Germans to avoid the bottleneck of traffic in Schonberg. In February 1945, Wood's body and that of another American soldier were found and a monument errected at the site. Around them were seven dead Germans. Wood was found to have money on him and his personal belongings, which would indicate he had fought to the death and had been the last to die.

In Schonberg at about 0830 the left hand force from the German 18th VGD coming up from Bleialf met with the right hand flooding down the River Our valley from the direction of Andler. This effectively cut off and encircled the two American regiments and their attachments up in the Eifel. Once the two German arms met at Schonberg the pressure seemed to ease. For now they were more concerned with their next objective – St Vith. The 18th Volksgrenadiers started to move cautiously west along the Schonberg-St.Vith road.

Troop B 18th Cavalry found themselves isolated once Schonberg was captured. Unable to rejoin the 423rd they were given permission to withdraw via Schonberg. Joining them was part of the 106th Recon Troop which had also become separated. The head of the column came out onto the Schonberg-Bleialf road from Amelschied. By mistake a Volkswagen full of grenadiers fell into the column. An American gunner in an armoured car noticed their mistake about the same time that they did – his reactions were quicker – he promptly shot up the vehicle and its occupants. The 3rd Platoon went down the road into Schonberg to ascertain the situation there. The M8 armoured cars crossed the Our river bridge and found the road blocked by a long line of American trucks. They saw the trucks were packed

German column on the move during the fighting.

with Germans; prisoners the cavalrymen thought, being taken to the rear. Then suddenly they noticed the Germans were armed. The three front M8's pulled over to the side of the road, then accelerated past the column of trucks, firing 37mm canister shot and machine guns into the soft-skinned vehicles. However, a MK IV tank rumbled out of a side road and knocked out the armoured cars. Only one got away to report back. Finding no other way out the cavalrymen destroyed their vehicles and formed themselves into small individual groups, split up and tried for St Vith on foot. About fifty actually made it.

Communications were erratic to say the least. The Germans were jamming all radio frequencies and it could take hours for a message to get through. One such message was sent by General Jones around about mid-morning to the two trapped regiments. It read, 'Expect to clear out area west of you this afternoon with reinforcements. Withdraw from present positions if they become untenable. Save all transportation possible.' Lieutenant-Colonel Cavender of the 423rd received this message at approximately 1500 but did not manage to relay it to Descheneaux until just after midnight. Also an airdrop of supplies and ammunition was promised to the beleaguered units and the drop co-ordinates given.

Descheneaux at 1610 sent a situation report to Division giving exact details of where his 422 Regiment was now placed. It did not arrive at St Vith until 2040.

The two regiments tightened themselves up and waited for the relief column to break through and the airdrop to materialize. Neither happened.

In Schonberg early that morning the Divisional Signal Officer Lieutenant-Colonel E. Williams and his wire chief, Master Sergeant C F Foster, were at the forward switching centre when the Germans suddenly appeared. They succeeded in sending a message back to Division reporting their plight before Williams had the switchboard destroyed. He sent his men west to St Vith after making sure everything was inoperative. Then he and Foster left under a hail of small-arms fire. They proceeded to Heuem where they found a mixture of personnel and a tank destroyer. Williams took charge and had the tank destroyer take up position to face in the direction of the pursuing German armour. As the first tank came into sight the tank destroyer let loose and stopped it dead. 'Time to go!' yelled Williams. They moved further west along the road, put the tank destroyer into another good position and began constructing a road-block with felled trees. They noticed that their own communication wires were still in place on posts beside the road and tapped into the phone line. Contacting 592nd FAB Williams called for artillery fire onto co-ordinates targeting the road down which the squeak and rattle of tank tracks could be heard. Only minutes passed before salvoes of 155mm shells screamed overhead and began saturating the road with high explosives between Schonberg and Heuem.

Colonel W Slayden, the assistant VIII Corp intelligence officer, had taken it upon himself to go out and find out exactly what was going on. His jeep had got as far as Heuem when he came under enemy small-arms fire. Turning around and heading back he joined up with Williams and his small party. This time Slayden tapped into the line and reported back that he was the last man between St Vith and Schonberg. All that morning they withdrew in a series of short hops carrying out a delaying action at each stage. The Volksgrenadiers kept up relentless advance.

That morning in St Vith, General Jones ordered Riggs to organize a task force and defend the town. At the same time he was given a reserve force in the form of the 168th Engineer Combat Battalion. This gave Riggs a small force consisting of remnants from his own 81st Engineers, the incomplete 168th and a token party of Headquarters personnel. His job was to hold the Germans back until CCB 7th Armored Division could arrive. Riggs relayed the orders to his new command and then set off for his command post in Heuem. About one mile east of St Vith atop a large hill Riggs met his own staff and part of the 168th command group, who had been chased out of Heuem by the oncoming enemy.

Riggs decided this was the place to dig in and make a stand. From this vantage point called the 'Prumerberg', good fields of fire could be had for at least 1000 yards down the Schonberg road. As units arrived from the Engineers, they were placed astride the road in a skirmish line. The men dug

'Dig in and wait for Heine to show.' Two GIs man a machine gun post.

General Bruce Clarke, defender of St Vith.

themselves in on a north-south line amongst the trees. A 'daisy chain' of mines was spread across the road and two bazooka teams placed in the woods covering the open ground. A 37mm anti-tank gun was on hand and set up. (This gun was put out of action in the first exchange of fire).

At about 1000 Brigadier General Bruce Clarke, commander of CCB 7th Armored Division, arrived at St Vith. Jones's command post was a hive of activity and everyone was relieved to see him. But, that soon turned to dismay when it was found that Clarke was very much the advance party and had no idea when his CCB would be with him – let alone General Hasbrouck with the rest of the 7th Armored Division. It was agreed that when the 7th arrived they would attack towards Schonberg, clear out that area, then move south and aid 9th Armored Division. That way it would free all the entrapped 106th regiments.

General Jones was looking and acting fairly calm, considering what was unfolding around him. He even mentioned to Middleton on the telephone, that there was no need for concern, 'We'll be all right when Clarke's troops arrive'.

But events were indicating the very opposite: early afternoon, in rushed Colonel Devine from the 14th Cavalry, so out of breath and panic stricken was he, he could barely blurt out that he had practically been 'chased into the building by a Tiger tank' and that they all ought to get out.

General Clarke knew he was looking at a broken man, who would be of no use at all to his unit. He turned to Jones and suggested he send Devine back to Middleton's headquarters in

Major General Alan W Jones

Bastogne, and perhaps there, would be able to give a first hand account of what was going on. Devine faded away.

A short time later the crackling of rifle fire was heard coming from the east. Jones and Clarke flew up to the top floor of the St Joseph Kloster (monastery) to take a look. It was here that Jones turned to Clarke and said,

'I've thrown in my last chips. I haven't got much, but your combat command is the one that will defend this position. You take over command of St Vith right now!'

General Jones was under enough stress already; his division was coming apart before his eyes, but to add to all this he had the added anguish of knowing that his only son, 1st Lieutenant Alan W Jones Jr, was with Colonel Cavender's 423rd Regiment stranded up there on the Schnee Eifel.

Clarke, with nothing else to do until his troops arrived, felt at a loose end. He proceeded to a crossroads just north of St Vith at the village of Rodt to await their arrival.

At about 1300, three enemy tanks and supporting infantry appeared in front of the 168th Engineers. One of the tanks slewed into a field, and the crew casually dismounted, whereupon they were promptly mowed down by a machine-gun crew. The second tank was disabled by a bazooka, and the third, along with the startled infantry, fled for cover back into the woods. This group tried again about an hour later but were driven off by the determined engineers. Riggs had managed to open up an air liaison radio circuit and contacted

Elements of the 7th Armored Division on the road.

a lone patrolling fighter, a rare bird in the low-ceiling
overcast of December 1944, when the weather had
successfully grounded the Allied airforce. This P47
Thunderbolt located the Germans after some low level
passes over the woods and strafed them several times,
inflicting heavy casualties on the hapless Germans.
Meanwhile General Clarke, on the lookout for the leading
elements of his division, had come across a monumental
traffic jam. Everything had come to a grinding halt. Vehicles
of every description were flowing west that day, away from
the front, some legitimately and others not. In fact it was
much the same on every road. The 7th Armored Division, on
its way to St Vith and its commander, General Clarke, found
itself bucking against this on-rushing tide of vehicles.

When at last they found each other Clarke, upon turning
and urging the leading elements of his division eastward,
found the route completely blocked by a retreating artillery
unit. The commander was threatening to shoot anybody who
interfered. Clarke in short order had the enraged commander
in front of him and yelled, 'You get your damned trucks off
this road, so my tanks can get up here. If there's any shooting
done around here, I'll start it'!

Elements of the 7th Armored Division began rolling into St
Vith; the 87th Cavalry Reconnaissance Squadron was the first

unit followed by Combat Command B. Troop B of the latter was sent straight out to reinforce the engineers on the Prumerberg. The rest of the squadron were to extend the line north, tie in with the 14th Cavalry, and screen the Wallerode area, which was now wide open to attack.

More elements of the 7th continued to arrive and irrespective of what they were, the units were sent piecemeal straight into the defence of St Vith. Much needed tanks were beginning to get through and were told to head up to the Prumerberg and report to Riggs for positioning. The cheers from the engineers as the tanks rolled up could almost be heard in St Vith.

The 38th Armored Infantry Battalion arrived, less one company and immediately went into the line east of the town. Commander of this unit was Lieutenant-Colonel William H. G Fuller, and on getting his men into position, he was given overall command of the eastern sector. Later that evening he was reinforced with Company A of the 31st Tank

40th Tank Battalion of the 7th Armored Division in position near St Vith.

Battalion and another company of infantry from the now arrived 23rd Armored Infantry Battalion (AIB). The rest of CCB was being put into an assembly area just west of St Vith.

Artillery was in short supply, as it was still held up on the clogged roads. Lieutenant-Colonel Roy U Clay of the 275th Armored Field Artillery Battalion, once attached to the 14th Cavalry found General Clarke, and told him he was sick of retreating, his guns were ready, and he wanted to shoot. He was welcomed with open arms.

By midnight 17 December most of CCB was in an arc from north of St Vith round to the south where it tied in with CCB 9th Armored Division and the 424th Infantry Regiment. It was soon pretty clear that no one was going to be able to counter-attack east to relieve the plight of the surrounded 422nd/423rd. St Vith itself was now under attack and all the forces would be needed to defend the town. It was also obvious that Germans were in full stream either side of St Vith, on their way to their own objectives deep into Belgium. The most serious threats were from the north and east – the defenders were in danger of being surrounded.

If the traffic jams and hold ups on the American side were bad, the Germans had it worse. Everything was being funnelled through gaps that had been cleared through the US lines. Panzers were being held up by horse drawn artillery, chaos was all around. The meticulous planning was going pear shaped. On the night of 17 December two high-ranking German officers became snarled up. General von Manteuffel, Commander 5th Panzer Army, was on his way forward to the headquarters of the 18th Volksgrenadier Division in Schonberg, firstly to see why St Vith had not yet fallen and secondly to put a bit of zest into their attack. At the same time, and on the same road, was Field Marshal Model, commander of Army Group B. They came upon each in the night beside the stalled traffic.

'And how is your situation, Baron?' asked Model.

Manteuffel replied 'Mostly good.'

'So? I got the impression you were lagging, especially in the St. Vith sector.'

'Yes,' said von Manteuffel, 'but we'll take it tomorrow.'

'I expect you to,' responded Model. 'And so that you'll take it quicker, tomorrow I'm letting you use the Führer Begleit Brigade.'

Monday 18 December 1944

General Jones surmised that if he could get his two entrapped regiments moving towards the west it would not only free them from their encirclement, but also help in the destruction of the enemy now on the outskirts of St Vith. At 0215 he sent a message by radio to the 422nd/423rd, telling them to shift northwest and, from their dug-in positions south of the Schonberg-St Vith road, destroy the enemy using that road. It was received by them at about 0400, Descheneaux bowed his head and almost sobbed, 'My poor men – they'll be cut to pieces'.

Both commanders of the 422nd/423rd agreed over the seriousness of the problem of communications between them. They decided to move out at dawn in column of Battalions the 423rd being nearer to the objective should lead. That was it as far as planning was concerned – no one

Men of the 422nd/423rd Regiments cut off and ordered to attack enemy traffic on the Schonberg-St Vith road.

coordinated anything else.

In fact the 422nd moved first. It was 0900 when the 2nd Battalion leading, started out across country towards the planned bivouac area in a narrow ravine just south of Skyline Drive, about one mile north of Oberlascheid. Here it was planned to stop for the night and get ready for the attack the following morning. The weather was thick fog and rain. It was hard going for the infantry slipping and sliding along through the myriad of forest tracks.

Boyd A Rutledge was in D Company (Heavy weapons) 1st Battalion, 422nd, he describes the move.

'The 422nd had no road access and had to make the entire trip cross country with no vehicles. 1st Battalion of the 422nd of which I was a member, started marching out at 1000 in the morning of the 18th and reached a position between Auw and Schonberg at 0100 the morning of the 19th. It got dark shortly after 1600, so nine hours of the journey was in the forest in the dark. We had to touch the pack of the man ahead in order to stay together. You could see absolutely nothing. In at least one place the pack of the man ahead of me all of a sudden disappeared followed by a muffled shout as he lost his footing. We were moving ninety percent of the time. I was carrying in my case full field pack and the bipod of my 81mm mortar up and down hills, through streams, mud, snow and we should have covered 15 or 20 miles. So after 15 hours of march our new position next morning, was by straight line only about three miles from the positions we abandoned. The historians show us moving in a slight arc to reach that position. It ain't true, and I don't believe anyone now knows the exact route. When an obstacle appeared, we veered off one way or the other, eventually to arrive at our position for the attack on the 19th. By that time, however, we were so exhausted that the excellent discipline exercised on the march evaporated and we were noisy when we finally reached our bivouac area. The Germans heard us and set up a defensive line a few hundred yards in front of us and awaited our attack in the morning dooming any chance of success.'

During that long march men had discarded equipment, the trails were littered with overcoats and gas mask bags. Also, men were beginning to wonder if it was a wise move. After all they had been safe in their well dug-in positions amongst the fortifications of the Siegfried Line. Now they were exposed to the elements. That night the men hunkered down as best they could, shivering and wishing they had not thrown away that overcoat. Descheneaux joined them in the bivouac area and was heard to say 'Where in the hell are we?' He told his Battalion commanders that they would advance next morning towards Hill 504 above Schonberg, 1st Battalion on the right, 2nd Battalion on left, and 3rd Battalion in reserve. They would capture Schonberg, move onto Heuem, and hopefully meet the expected relief forces coming from St Vith. Up to now, apart from the 1st Battalion having a few skirmishes on the right flank they had encountered no opposition.

But it had been enough for the Germans to suspect that the Americans were on the move.

Meanwhile, the 423rd started at about 1000, 2nd Battalion leading, followed by 3rd Battalion and the 1st Battalion bringing up the rear, along with the regimental vehicles and artillery. The route to be taken was Halenfeld – Oberlascheid

Men of the 106th Division on the move.

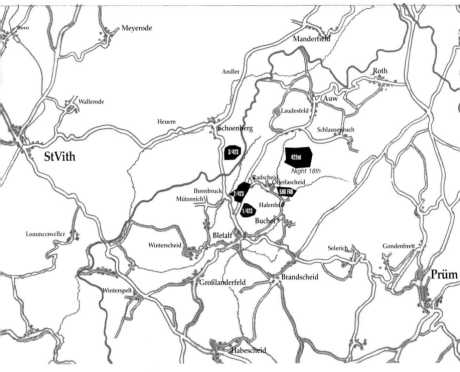

422nd/423rd positions 18th December 1944

– Radscheid – Engineers Cut-off and on to Schonberg.

At about midday Colonel Puett's 2nd Battalion had reached Skyline Drive at Radscheid, and immediately started receiving heavy fire from his left flank, from the direction of '88 Corner'. Puett immediately turned his Battalion in that direction to meet the threat. The ground was very open, but the infantry, supported by machine guns and mortars, attacked down either side of Skyline Drive to try and clear the area. The Germans were reinforcing the sector all the time from Bleialf, as they needed to keep the route open. Puett called Cavender for aid, and recommended to his Regimental Commander that he commit another Battalion to counter-attack. By this time most of the 2nd Battalion was pinned to the ground between Radscheid and '88 Corner'.

It was about this time that another message reached

Cavender which superseded the previous plan. Now Division wanted them to advance directly at Schonberg; there was not going to be any counter-attack by the 7th Armored Division, they were to do it all by themselves. Cavender sent a messenger to Descheneaux with the new orders. He then ordered his 3rd Battalion, commanded by Lieutenant-Colonel Earl F. Klinck, to side slip the 2nd Battalion and head north-west. This they did. The Battalion crossed Skyline Drive just above Radscheid, and followed a secondary track down to the Ihrenbach stream. Having crossed this, the Battalion suddenly came under small-arms fire. Managing to avoid a fight, the men climbed the hill and plodded on north west until Company L, with Company K supporting, actually made contact with the Bleialf-Schonberg road to the left of of Hill 536 (Lindscheid Hill). This hill is just south of Hill 504 which directly overlooks Schonberg. Company L drew fire from German anti-aircraft guns being used in the ground role and small arms fire. At this point Lieutenant-Colonel Klinck stopped and dug in for the night. Much to his surprise a large portion of Company F, 422nd joined him, they had over shot their bivouac, some one and a half miles away to the south-east. Things were beginning to get hopelessly mixed up.

He sent runners back to Cavender to tell him of his position – they never got there.

In response to Puett's request for help, Cavender sent the 1st Battalion under Lieutenant-Colonel William H. Craig as reinforcements. It was now dusk, and the 1st Battalion could make little headway. Confusion set in. Both were told to withdraw to the vicinity of Oberlascheid ready for the move north.The 2nd Battalion had suffered over 300 casualties, and had expended the majority of its ammunition. The 1st Battalion had lost 70 men and was also low on ammunition. The wounded had to be left, along with the medics attending them.

Kenneth Hunt a medic with the 423rd stayed behind with the wounded.

'On both the 16th and 17th I spent most of my time helping carry litter cases to the aid station from various

positions on the field. I was exposed to enough cold and snow to develop frostbite in both feet. By 18 December, we were treating about 25 or 30 wounded Americans. We had also captured four Germans who were only slightly wounded. What I remember about them is that they were very young, about 16 or so. They were smiling and joking among themselves. The war was over for them, they were going to an "American rest camp". Most of our men had severe wounds. Some had been hit in the stomach or chest. We were cut off from the Battalion field hospital so they couldn't be sent back there. And many would not survive the ordeal of moving with the regiment. The best decision was to leave them in the aid station with enough supplies to last a few days and to return for them as soon as possible. Major Fridline asked for two medics to stay with the wounded. It was no problem for me to decide to stay behind. My feet were really giving me trouble. I knew that I could never keep up if we had to make a forced march. Major Fridline made sure that we were left with

Tending a wounded GI during the Battle of the Bulge.

plenty of bandages, plasma, and drugs. He told us not to spare the morphine to relieve pain.'

Kenneth Hunt went on to say,

> *'Soon we heard vehicles, tanks and trucks going along the road. I looked out the window and saw the entire German army passing by. Our patients in the basement could hear but not see the commotion. "Whats going on out there?" they asked. "Those are our men," I replied. "They'll pick us up as soon as they can." It was not until the 4th day that we heard a loud knock on the door. By that time our supplies were running out and our morale was low. Some of the men were in very bad shape.'*

Hunt was hoping some kind Germans might pass by and take every one to a clean hospital. On opening the door to check that the Red Cross flag was still in place, he was faced with the muzzle of a rifle.

> *'They ordered that I raise my hands while they searched for weapons. When they discovered that I wasn't armed, they relaxed a bit. The sergeant said, "Don't you Americans know that you should be home for Christmas?" He laughed sarcastically. Those were the only English words he knew. "Do you have any wounded Germans inside?" the officer asked. "Yes, four." "Let us see them." We went into the basement. When our men saw the Germans they were silent. Even the German wounded looked grim. "How have you been treated?" the officer asked. One of the Germans replied, "The medics treated us just like their own men. They even gave us white bread to eat." The next four days which followed were among the saddest in my life. The Germans tossed the American wounded in a truck without regard to the seriousness of their wounds and drove off over an unpaved road. I am sure that many of them did not survive the trip.'*

Cavender moved his command post from Oberlascheid up to just north of Radscheid into the original positions of the 590th FAB before the 16th Dec. At 2200 Cavender sent a patrol north to try and locate the lost 3rd Battalion. This, the patrol found dug in on the side of the hill, but the vehicles of the Battalion had bogged down and were stuck in the Ihrenbach stream. Cavender sent patrols east to try and

GIs in make-shift camouflage white sheets.

locate the 422nd Regiment but to no avail. At this moment the radio waves became clear and unjammed. Word came through from division. A food and ammunition air-drop was to take place near the bend on the Schonberg road close to where the 3rd Battalion was situated. Then Division sent an irritating message to the 423rd. In fact it was the last message they were to receive:

> 'Attack Schonberg, do maximum damage to enemy there, then attack towards St.Vith. This mission is of gravest importance to the nation. Good luck.'

After all, were they not doing their very best anyway?

Cavender, message in hand went forward to find Klinck's 3rd Battalion. He found them dug in, and decided to pull all his regiment forward to that position, ready for an attack on Schonberg the following morning. The 1st and 2nd Battalions had disengaged and moved across the Ihrenbach stream. 1st Battalion left one company in the Oberlaschied area to cover the withdrawal. The two Battalions took up their positions behind the 3rd Battalion, but on the reverse side of Hill 536. This was achieved by the early hours of the 19th, the men were tired soaked and hungry. That night in pitch darkness the 590th FAB had followed the regimental vehicles down the improvised trail into the Ihrenbach valley, about an hour before dawn the 2.5 ton GMCs came to a grinding halt, the way blocked by the abandoned vehicles of the infantry. The artillerymen, totally exhausted, slept in their trucks the best

Attacking German grenadiers of the 18 VGD fire on the US lines.

they could and awaited daybreak. The position at the end of the night of 18 December left both regiments not knowing where each other were; the 423rd was consolidated on the hill just south of Schonberg, the 422nd were encamped in a ravine not far away, south of Skyline Drive.'

In the north, General Josef 'Sepp' Dietrich's Sixth Panzer Army had met unexpected resistance in the Elsenborn ridge area. It now began to flow south to avoid it.

Needing to get back on track for the Meuse River objective it could do little else but touch on the St Vith area.

The town was hit from three directions that day. The 18th VGD Mobile Battalion streamed out of the woods from Wallerode and onto the main highway that leads into St Vith. At the same time the 1st SS Panzergrenadier Regiment struck at the village of Hunningen only one mile north. The Engineers up on the Prumerberg heights were hit again. All these attacks were driven back by determined efforts from the US defenders. St Vith had now become a finger stuck into the German attack.

General Hasbrouck had arrived with the rest of the 7th Armored Division and he established his headquarters in the Middle School on the Rue de l'Hotel de Ville, in Vielsalm. With him came Combat Command R which he sent to defend the north of St Vith. His Combat Command A was

General Robert Hasbrouck

put into reserve to the south-west, but soon the majority of this unit was thrown into the fray to help the hard pushed northern flank. Because of the pressure on the area, General Jones and his staff also moved back to Vielsalm and established themselves there. General Clarke moved his command post to Crombach where he still directed the defence of St Vith itself. All through the day the Germans exerted pressure on the town, but each time tanks and infantry were rushed to the trouble spots to meet the German threats head on.

One quiet area that day was the north-eastern sector. The highlight came when an M8 armoured car that was concealed in the woods noticed to its front a Tiger tank passing along a fire break in the trees. After the tank passed the M8 roared out of its hiding place and proceeded to catch the tank up from the rear. The Tiger's commander standing in the turret spotted the armoured car and desperately tried to get his 88mm gun round to bear. The tiny M8, with its driver's foot pressed to the floor, closed within range and let off three 37mm shells, striking the Tigers thin rear plate. The tank shuddered, there was a hollow explosion, flames and smoke poured from the crippled beast. The impudent little M8 returned to its original hide-out, triumphant.

A Tiger rolling through the wooded Ardennes.

CHAPTER FIVE

THE INEVITABLE
Surrender

Tuesday 19th December 1944

As daylight began to show through the dark woods south of Schonberg, the infantry of the 423rd began to reorganize. The 3rd Battalion was the furthest forward. Behind it the somewhat depleted 1st Battalion and the 2nd Battalion were in position on the reverse slope of Hill 536.

The 590th FAB found themselves in a narrow valley. Steep, densely wooded slopes rose up on either side. There was swampy ground to their right front, and flowing directly across their path was a stream some six or eight feet wide. The infantry, unable to get its vehicles across the stream during the night, had abandoned them completely blocking the way. The infantry which had been protecting them had forged ahead, there was little else they could do but get themselves into position where they sat. Guns were unhitched, A and C Batteries were forward near the stream, while B Battery was about 200 yards to the rear around a curve in the wood line. They would still be able to support the infantry's attack, although ammunition was now in short supply. An aid station had been set up in the scrub pine along the lower edge of the far slope.

To their right, but unknown to them, Descheneaux's 422nd Regiment also readied itself for the coming attack. He had learned of the new orders the previous night and had assembled his Battalion commanders for briefing. His plan was to attack the wooded height (Hill 504) above Schonberg with two Battalions forward and one held in reserve. He knew he had no artillery for support but there was still some mortar ammunition on hand. Descheneaux had no idea where the exact location of his sister regiment was but assumed it would be attacking on his left at the same time.

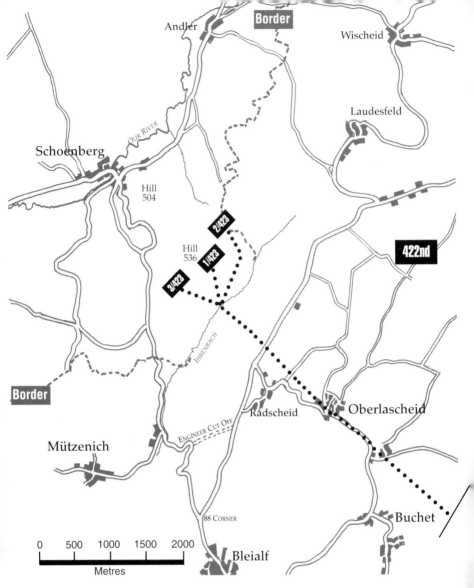

422/423 Positions prior to attack on Schonberg

At 0830 Cavender began briefing his Battalion commanders. Klinck's 3rd Battalion was to make the main effort and attack down the road to Schonberg. The 1st and 2nd Battalions would be to the right and attack over Hill 504 and down into the village. They started synchronizing their watches, Cavender announced 'It is now exactly 9:00

o'clock'. As if that had been the signal the Germans had been waiting for they let loose a tremendous artillery barrage which swept the hill. Everyone scattered, trying to find cover. Lieutenant-Colonel Craig, commander of the 1st Battalion, was killed.

The shelling lasted for about thirty minutes, as it lifted a commotion was heard from the rear. The Germans' shells had caught the artillerymen tightly packed in the valley. Totally defenceless and with machine-gun fire now coming at them from the heights, the 590 FAB could do little else but destroy its weapons and surrender.

The 18th Volksgrenadiers had moved in behind.

For the 423rd there was now only one way to go and that was forward. What vehicles remained were promptly ordered destroyed.

At 1000, what was left of the infantry Battalions jumped off, Klinck's 3rd Battalion took off quickly, Company L of that Battalion moved on up the Schonberg road supported by machine-gun fire from part of Company M's heavy weapons.

John Kline from Company M remembers being told to take his 30 calibre water-cooled machine gun and to place it

Hastily dug machine-gun post with a .30 calibre water-cooled Browning mg in position.

in the edge of the woods in a direction that he took to be Schonberg. His position was a considerable distance up the hill.

'I was not in an area that was receiving small-arms fire, but all of our exposure was to heavy artillery. In fact, once during the day, there was a piece of shrapnel that hit beside my position, close enough that I reached out and touched it, it was at least ten centimetres across and 50-60 centimetres long. It had spent most of its energy, but made a terrifying sound as it came through the trees and hit near me.'

From his position John Kline could see Company L way below him caught in the ditches on the side of the road. He could hear the screams for help and shouts for 'Medics' as they were being torn apart. Unfortunately his machine gun was too far back to help the infantry. He could not move either because the same artillery was hitting him.

Another witness to the events taking place commented:

'Company L was being slaughtered. A sniper was killing a lot of them. We had spotted the sniper, nearby, in a clump of bushes. The range was too short for the elevating mechanism. My squad leader (mortars) was trying to elevate the mortar, by holding it vertically. He was killed by a bullet in the temple. Another mortar man and I grabbed the mortar and dropped three shells in the area of the sniper, killing him.'

It was not long before they ran straight into heavy fire from German 88's and 40mm anti-aircraft guns being used in a ground role. An American Sherman tank came around the sharp hairpin bend, the GIs thinking this was part of the relieving armour began to stand up, to their horror the tank raked them with machine-gun fire, then withdrew, it had been captured by the Germans. At the same instant the rear of the company was attacked by an estimated German rifle company, which was moving up from the Bleialf area. Captain J. S Huyatt, commander of Company L, detached part of his force to turn around and counter-attack the Germans coming from his rear. This they did and actually drove the Germans back. Through this action, Huyatt's Company had become separated from the remainder of the Battalion. He managed to get what was left of it, some forty men, up the side of the hill and dug in.

The Germans came back with a vengeance. By 1330 the remnants of Company L, surrounded and out of ammunition, could do nothing else but surrender. Companies I and K of the same Battalion moved on towards Schonberg, they actually reached the southern outskirts of the village before they too were stopped by intense direct anti-aircraft artillery fire.

By 1500 Lieutenant-Colonel Klinck could get no further, he pulled the two battered companies back up the slopes of Hill 504.

The 1st Battalion added little to the attack from the beginning. Its commander had been killed during the morning's briefing, so no word had reached the Battalion on what they were supposed to do. Luckily the executive officer, Major C. H. Cosby took command, collected the orders, and proceeded to cross the line of departure almost on time, but with what. Company A was lost in the Oberlascheid area from the previous day, Company D had been caught fully in

Surrounded and out of ammunition American soldiers began coming down from the hills.

the morning barrage, had taken many casualties, and also was as good as lost. As the Battalion headed for its jump off position Company C was earmarked for regimental rearguard. So Cosby led the 1st Battalion, in reality now Company B and part of Battalion Headquarters Company, along the eastern slope of Hill 504. Through the thick woods and under constant mortar and artillery fire they pushed forward, finally reaching the road running north out of Schonberg. Here Company B dug in, the headquarters company had become separated and was now lost. Under constant fire they were finally forced to surrender when enemy tanks overran their positions. By 1400 the 1st Battalion had been eliminated.

Lieutenant Austin Sellery, M Company 423rd recalled, 'Memories about the events that preceded our capture on 19 December, 1944, are rather vague. I recall receiving orders to pull off the line and proceed towards Schonberg on 18 December. When night came we were on a wooded knoll and were told to dig our mortars in. Tree roots and frozen ground made this impossible. Throughout the night we could hear Germans around us. I was amazed at how casual they were in making their presence known. We were told the plan was to jump off at 0900 hours. This was impossible against the Germans overwhelming fire power. Captain Hardy was killed and Lieutenant Weigers was seriously injured within yards of me. It looked certain that we would all be killed and all that was left was for us to fight until we ran out of ammunition. Our remaining senior officer surrendered us to the Germans about 4.00 pm that afternoon.'

The last remaining Battalion in the 423rd was the 2nd. Lieutenant-Colonel J. F Puett led his Battalion forward to the right of the 1st. He soon came up alongside the 1st at a distance of about five hundred yards but separated by a steep ravine, known as Linne Creek. At 1300, knowing that the other two Battalions were being held up by enemy fire, Puett sent a message to Cavender asking permission to be allowed to attack Schonberg from the north east and relieve the pressure. By 1400 he still had not heard anything and realized that communications were virtually impossible

After months of bad news the German people were to be treated to the sight of American prisoners in the propaganda newsreels.

because of the thick woods and hilly terrain. He gave orders to attack at 1430. His men were getting ready, when suddenly they came under small-arms fire from their right rear. It was part of the 422nd Regiment who had mistaken Puett's Battalion for Germans. Although it was only a matter of minutes before aggresive company commanders rectified the situation, his plans had been severely disrupted. During this reorganization Puett sent patrols out to his front and right. At 1515 these patrols returned whilst Puett was in conference with Descheneaux. They both learnt that to their right there were 35 enemy tanks and several self-propelled guns, and to their front there were strong German armoured forces with artillery going into position. Out of touch with his own regiment Puett decided to join forces with the 422nd

The 422nd Regiment left their bivouac area at about 0730 that morning. The 1st Battalion on the right, now led by Major W. P Moon owing to the original commander Lieutenant-Colonel T Kent being killed on the Schnee Eifel, crossed Skyline Drive. They were immediately hit by fire from assault guns and infantry. Companies A and B didn't even make it out of the assembly area, they were stopped dead by the sheer force of the German presence. Many of these men were caught in a narrow ravine which led to Skyline Drive, with Germans at either end, and the men bottled up, there was sheer slaughter. However some men from Company C did manage to cross the road and went on to gain a small open height beyond it. These men also received attention from the same Germans from the direction of Auw. Only one platoon managed to get to the assigned area, the high ground beyond the Ihrenbach stream.

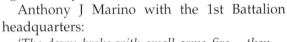

Anthony J Marino with the 1st Battalion headquarters:

Anthony J Marino

'The dawn broke with small-arms fire – then the crack-crack of 88s from Panzer tanks. A Lieutenant came over the hill – he had a rifle bullet go through his forearm. A cry rose up "bazooka ammunition – has anyone got bazooka ammo"? Our Battalion had no support heavy weapons aside from bazookas, and ammunition was sparse, only what men could carry. Also when our bullets were initially expended we were out. The firing lasted for a short time. Then I saw our line companies in rout – running into the ravine upon my left, I could plainly see our infantrymen running for cover. However, with 88s falling in their midst it was a turkey shoot for the Panzers. Then a cry – "surrender". The 88's stopped. Men were surrendering. I asked "what do I do"? Captain Mohne told me to destroy my weapon and map case. Then they went off. I buried my map case and destroyed my M1 and pistol, flinging the parts as far as I could. I then went down the hill to join with the surrendering troops'.

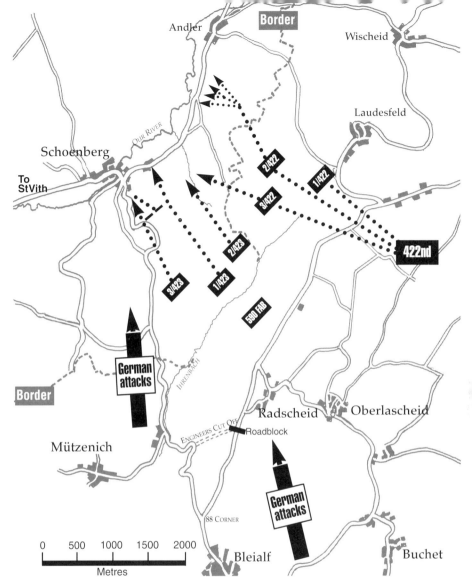

Attacks by the 106th Division, 19 December 1944.

The 2nd Battalion to the left of the 1st did manage to get across Skyline Drive in some order, although they did receive fire upon leaving. Companies E, G and H pushed on to where the platoon from Company C was. Company F of this Battalion had got lost the night before and had somehow joined up with Klinck's 3rd Battalion.

The men pushed on and finally reached the high ground

overlooking the Schonberg-Andler road. Descheneaux joined his men there. Looking down to the road they saw it packed 'bumper to bumper' with vehicles. This at long last must be the relief column they thought, or at least vehicles of the 423rd. The dream bubble was quick to burst when they were spotted by vigilant Germans. In a matter of seconds flak half-tracks raked the hill side where they stood.

Company H with its mortars and machine guns began to take on the Germans from the very top of the slope, and started scoring some hits. But before too long the accuracy of the German gunners proved too much. What was left of the three battered companies hauled themselves over the slope to comparative safety and took stock.

Lastly the 3rd Battalion, Lieutenant-Colonel D. F. Thompson led his men across Skyline Drive to the left of the 2nd Battalion, and into the woods of the Linne Creek. His men spotted movement to their left front and immediately opened fire, this was of course Puett's 2nd Battalion they had seen.

Unable to move in any direction Descheneaux started to form a semblance of a perimeter defence. He now realized the situation was hopeless, wounded men were everywhere, there was no fresh water and no one had eaten anything substantial for some time, ammunition was just about spent. With head bowed he conferred with his battalion commanders and decided to surrender. It was 1600, Descheneaux sent out the white flag, he was not going to waste any more lives needlessly.

Puett, still very much active had been out patrolling, when he returned he learned that the surrender was about to take place, and asked Descheneaux if he could try and lead his battalion to safety, this was overruled on the grounds that it might draw unnecessary fire. Puett went back to his men and told them that if anybody wanted to go they could. A few did drift away. At 1700 when the Germans came up to the heights to take them prisoner, Puett had only 387 men and 14 officers left in his Battalion.

It was at about the same time the same conclusion was arrived at in the 423rd area.

Colonel Cavender had moved his command post up to the 3rd Battalion on Hill 504 and had made contact with the 422nd by patrol. With one of his battalions eliminated and one out of his control, overwhelming German forces and artillery building up all the time to his front and rear things looked bleak. The hill was continually being raked by artillery, mortar and machine-gun fire, casualties were getting heavier by the minute and there was just no way of caring for them properly. Ammunition had just about run out, no food or water. Cavender would not sacrifice any more lives, he told the men that they could try and get out in small groups if they so wished, few made it.

At 1630 on the 19th December Cavender surrendered his Regiment.

An excerpt from John Kline's wartime diary reads:

German six-barrelled mortar, the Nebelwerfer – known to the Americans as the 'Screaming Meemie'.

'The woods and open areas on the slope leading to the road, was littered with dead and wounded. Some time between 1600 and 1630 a American officer, accompanied by a German officer told us we were surrounded. He told us that we were cut off from the other Regiment, the 422nd, and that our Regimental commander, Colonel C. C. Cavender, was ordering us to surrender. We disabled our weapons by breaking them on tree trunks or by taking them apart and throwing the parts in different directions. After that the Germans led us to a clearing in the forest and directed us to throw down our equipment, eg: ammo belts, packs, hand-grenades and trench-knives. I quickly disposed of the German binoculars that I had found earlier. We were led in a small column down to the Schonberg-Bleialf road in front of the rifle companies. There were Germans on one side of the road and Americans on the other. They had been facing each other, in a fierce fire fight, from ditch to ditch. There were many dead, both Americans and Germans. The wounded were still crying for help.

'As we approached the Schonberg road, it seemed that hundreds of Germans rose up out of the field. There was a German truck burning in the middle of the road. Behind the truck was an American infantryman lying in the road. He was dressed like an officer, but with no insignia, as would be normal in combat. He was wearing his winter uniform, a heavy winter coat, ammo belt and canteen. He was lying on his back, as if he were resting. The body had no head or neck. It was as if somebody had sliced it off with a surgical instrument, leaving no sign of blood. We were then walked in columns to Bleialf, where they herded us into a church courtyard.'

As the weary, hungry men of the 422nd/423rd came down from the heights overlooking Schonberg, almost all of them felt let down and bewildered. Let down because of all the false promises, and bewildered through having to take on such an impossible task. Some did escape, at least for a while. Remnants of both regiments drifted back generally in a south easterly direction.

Second Lieutenant L. R. Walker of Company H, 422nd led

a column of men away from the inferno. More men joined him, some from the 423rd, 81st Engineers, artillery and even anti-aircraft units. When he felt safe to do so he took stock, there were men from 15 different companies and six basic units. Keeping on the move they came across the 422nd's motor pool and supply base just before dark. This was situated just south west of Laudesfeld near Hill 576. Here the men dug in and formed a perimeter defence. In came Major Ouellette, 2nd Battalion 422nd's Executive Officer, and Major Moon, commander of the 1st Battalion 422nd. In all, about 500 men gathered from all over the area. A little food and some ammunition was foraged and by nightfall the men were established. The Germans were quick to discover that there was still a pocket of resistance and proceeded to shower the area with artillery. There were a few casualties but the GIs had dug in well and had covered their fox holes with logs and dirt. Exchanges of rifle fire with the nearby Germans were frequent. Across the valley came the strains of popular American music being played by a German sound truck. In between songs there were demands for surrender and of how nice it would be to play baseball in the comfort of a prison camp. Soon after noon the following day, Staff Sergeant Richard Thomas could take no more of it. Rounding up a few volunteers he led out a patrol, and put paid to the mobile propaganda machine once and for all with a couple of well thrown hand-grenades.

A German reconnaisance car approached from the direction of Laudesfeld, with German medics on board and an American medic from the 423rd. They met with Majors Oullette and Moon and said they wanted a temporary truce to open up the road network within the area to allow evacuation of wounded from both sides. The two Majors decided to send Lieutenant Houghton of Company D along with them to make sure there was going to be no monkey business. The troops withheld their fire until Houghton returned at about 1830. With him he brought an ultimatum of surrender before 2100 from the Germans. Houghton told of artillery and massed German troops waiting to saturate the area. A conference between the American officers confirmed

Lieutenant Long brought his Intelligence and Reconnaissance Platoon through the German lines and safely into St Vith where he told of the surrender of two regiments of the 106th Division.

that it was useless and futile to hold out against such overwhelming odds. Word was got to the Germans that they would surrender at 0800 the next day. Although the Germans were not happy about this, obviously because it was tying up vital manpower needed elsewhere, reluctantly they consented. Major's Oullette and Moon needed the extra time to give the men a decent rest and to be able to scrounge what food and extra clothing might be about.

At 0800, 21 December with weapons and vehicles destroyed, (against the German wishes), the last men from the 422nd/423rd Regiments went reluctantly into captivity.

Some men did make it out. Lieutenant Ivan H. Long and his Intelligence and Reconnaissance Platoon had been holding a road block outside Radscheid. They found themselves surrounded. With some other men from different units joining all the time, Lieutenant Long decided to head north, skirt around Schonberg and then make towards the west. They destroyed what vehicles they had with them and set off on foot, approximately forty men in all. Hiding by day in the thick forests and moving silently by night with the aid of a compass, the tired, dirty men entered the St Vith salient on the 21st December. There, they told the story of the two regiments surrendering. After being fed and allowed to rest they went straight back into the line again up on the Prumerberg.

A deadly silence now hung over the area. At last Field Marshal Model and Sepp Dietrich in their respective command posts in the tiny village of Meyerode could now get on with the task in hand.

General Hoffmann-Schonborn's 18th VGD were, on this day, more concerned with eliminating the Schnee Eifel threat, which had plagued them from the beginning. He could not concentrate on St Vith until the two US regiments were finally eradicated. However, artillery was being brought up in vast amounts to the St Vith area. The American defenders were constantly being shelled and mortared. Other formations came drifting in and were joining in with the defenders.

To the Germans, the fall of St Vith was crucial, already well behind in their timed schedule, things were going seriously wrong. In order to achieve success, the road network in the area must be secured otherwise the entire assault was in jeopardy, the breakthrough in the north had been stemmed by determined American forces on the Elsenborn Ridge, forcing the II SS Panzer Corps south. Unless this unit could break through and get behind the US lines all would be lost. St Vith must now fall in order to unleash the Panzers. German troops were probing all around the US perimeter, (now very much a salient), in order to try and find a soft spot to assault.

It is not my intention to delve to deeply into the actual assault on St Vith as this would take the tour beyond the scope of this book. It would be sufficient enough at this stage to say that all the outlying villages played a crucial part in the Battle for St Vith. Each one would have its own story to tell both by the particular US unit defending, or the German unit attacking, of which there were many. Like Bastogne, but unfortunately not so well publicized, but equally as

A King Tiger passes a column of American prisoners.

important, St Vith was virtually surrounded. The valiant defenders gave their all, against superior numbers and probably the best the Germans had to offer at that time.

By 21 December, the major forces in the eleven by ten mile salient included, 7th A.D Combat Command A, B and R, Combat Command B of the 9th A.D, 424th Infantry Regiment of the 106th Division, 81st and 168th Engineers and the newly arrived 112th Infantry Regiment from the now split 28th Division, plus numerous other smaller units including artillery, anti-aircraft and tank destroyers.

Colossal German forces were now poised for the final onslaught, the 18th VGD with tanks from the Führer Escort Brigade directly in front of St Vith, the 62nd VGD with tanks to the south, and the 9th and 2nd SS Panzer Divisions from the II Panzer Corps skirmishing around the northern sector.

After a tremendous barrage German troops and tanks

After the Americans had pulled back from St Vith this important junction of roads was heavily bombed.

St Vith in January 1945.

attacked from the three sides. The line held yet they tried again and again. Finally, the superior German forces broke the American resistance that evening. General Clarke, seeing that his forces could no longer hold, withdrew his men west of St Vith. A lot of men were trapped unable to withdraw, these were instructed to regroup and attack back through the town to rejoin the new forming line. For many it was just impossible. Lieutenant-Colonel Riggs found himself with about seventy men, too few by half to do any real damage. He told the men to split into small groups and make it back the best they could. Just about all of them, including Riggs, were captured.

Although St Vith itself was now in German hands, they were still being stalled by the fact that the Americans had formed another defensive position. This time it became known as 'The Fortified Goose Egg', due to its shape.

It soon became clear that another encirclement of American forces would soon take place. At 0900 on 22 December orders were issued for the withdrawal of all forces within the 'Goose Egg' across the River Salm and into the relative safety of the newly arrived 82nd Airborne Division. The way out was by means of forest roads, much of them muddy, slushy and impassable. Men not manning the front lines were employed in desperately trying to make good the roads.

General Montgomery, now in charge of the northern section and Allied troops, sent General Hasbrouck a message saying, 'You have accomplished your mission – a mission well-done. It is time to withdraw'.

That night someone must have been smiling on the ravished Americans. It froze and froze hard. The once boggy ground became rock solid. The difficult withdrawal took place, it was now or never. The well disciplined men executed the manouevre, some 22,000 of them. It was not for the feint hearted.

The building in the foreground had been used as 106th Division HQ.

Gunners of the 7th Armored Division provide the first line of defence during the battle.

As the men were reaching the comparative safety of the west bank of the Salm river, General Jones of the 106th Division, so over-worked in his first time in combat finally collapsed. He had suffered a heart attack.

St Vith would stay in German hands until 23 January, 1945, when ironically the 7th Armored Division, supported by the 424th Infantry Regiment to its north, attacked back through the town. After many days of hard combat the ground was regained. They found the town flattened, the airforce had bombed it severely to try and stop the German advance.

The 106th Division in that first week of combat had lost some 416 men killed in action, 1,246 wounded and 7,001 missing in action. Over 60 percent of the division's personnel were dead, wounded or captured.

Unknown to the men of the division at the time, they had done exactly what was needed of them. They stalled the offensive. The Germans had been so held up by the stubborn resistance on the Schnee Eifel, and on the route to St Vith, that the offensive could not possibly have succeeded.

CHAPTER SIX

THE AFTERMATH
Prisoners of War

With darkness falling, the men being brought down from the heights were herded into assembly areas allocated by the Germans. Senior officers were interrogated at Kessler's dance hall in Andler by SS officers. Many men were marched to Bleialf where they spent their first night in captivity, shivering and huddled together for warmth in the church yard. The German propaganda photographers had a field day showing the dejected beaten Americans. Great emphasis was made on showing blacks and whites together to give the idea to the German people what a rotten mixture the American army was. At the same time hundreds of other bewildered men were marched to the rail centres of Prum and Gerolstein. Almost all had been relieved of their personnel belongings and much of their warm clothing. Throughout the cold wet night they trudged into Germany. All were already exhausted due to lack of sleep during the last three days of combat. The majority of them had not eaten nor had a drink in the last twenty-four hours, and it did

Nazi propaganda made great play on the mixture to be encountered in the American army and how it was proving detrimental to that nation's fighting skills.

not look to them as though the Germans were going to give them anything. Men began to drink melted snow or even ditch water to satisfy their thirsts brought on by the constant marching.

Anthony J. Marino was one of these prisoners of war:

'We moved for the full day toward a small town. Then we were rested in the early evening and marched further. Late that evening many of us were billeted in a factory or warehouse – most of the men having to settle out in open fields in the snow. Then we were fed hard crackers and yellow cheese. I slept on a shelf for the night. At dawn we were on the march again, all day and into the night. We were assembled into boxcars at a railroad siding.'

J. Don Holtzmuller, of the 589th FAB, has hazy recollections of the journey to the POW:

'The first town we passed through was Prum. There, a German officer made me give my rubber overshoes to a German infantryman. The first night we slept in a German bunker on the Siegfried Line. While marching back into Germany we passed a plethora of German war equipment along the roads. Many tanks (Tigers and Panthers), trucks, trucks pulling trucks, cannons of all varieties, horse drawn equipment, and armaments and equipment made in all the countries of Europe. Another night we slept in a big warehouse. At one stop we were made to give up one of our outer coats. Unfortunately for me, they took my overcoat, which left me with just a thin field jacket. As it was getting colder every day, I found I was under-dressed. I had taken off my long underwear the day before the battle and was wearing summer underwear when I was captured. Food during these days was practically nil. Water was also scarce and once I drank water scooped out of a roadside ditch with a dirty helmet liner. We were locked in rail cars with no heat or toilet facilities. It was frightfully cold.'

The railway box cars proved a terrible experience for the men. Designed to carry forty men or eight horses, the Golden Lions found themselves jammed packed into the small boxes on four spindly wheels, anything up to eighty to a truck! The floors were covered with a thin layer of straw, many still contained dung from their previous cargo of horses. With no toilet facilities, men had to use their helmets. These were then passed from one man to another towards a small air vent, where they were emptied and passed back. Water was obtained by collecting the condensation which built up inside the wagon or by licking the ice covered steel hinges.

It was hardly surprising that the already weakened men became disease-ridden. Dysentery became rife.

The train journeys were long and slow, often they were shunted into sidings to allow more important trains to pass. The tracks were constantly destroyed by bombing, so long and difficult detours were taken to avoid damaged areas. Then there was the fear of being attacked by the Allied Airforce. The British and American pilots liked nothing better than to 'beat-up' German trains.

Men began to arrive at the prison camps, officers and enlisted men were segregated.

J Don Holtzmuller arrived at the town of Hammelburg,

'We detrained and marched up a big hill to German Prison Camp XIII-C. Thus, on 26 December, 1944, my 128 days of incarceration in a German prison camp began. We were put in wooden barracks that housed about 80 men. We were given a small piece of German black bread and tin bowl filled with a hot liquid which tasted somewhat like tea. I drank the tea, but the bread tasted so bad that I couldn't eat it and I gave it away. In a couple of days this bread started to taste like cake! We kept the tin bowl we had been given and this became our eating vessel for the rest of our captivity. Our living quarters

Stalag IX Bad-Orb, Germany, one of the camps used to take 106th Division men.

were similar to those portrayed on the TV show "Hogan's Heroes". The wooden bunks were three high with a thin mattress made of burlap and filled with very little straw. Very few wooden slats supported the mattress. Prisoners, to try to warm the building burned a few slats in some bunks. We found out later that it was a crime against the German State to burn bed slats. The next morning we were assembled outside and the Germans sorted us out; first the black soldiers and the Jewish soldiers were segregated. Initially they thought I was black. The last boxcar in which I had travelled had been carrying what I suppose was black graphite and I was covered with this black material. I had to roll up my sleeve to show I was white. The privates were then taken away. Per the Geneva Convention, privates could be made to work on non-war production jobs and they were put out on what was called Kommandos to do farm work or the like. In a couple of days we non-commissioned officers, corporals and sergeants were moved to new barracks. Our new quarters consisted of a large brick building which had been a horse stable. This area had been a training camp for German soldiers. There were three of these buildings, one above the other on the side of a steep hill. High, triple barbed wire fences surrounded the barracks with watchtowers at the corners. Ten feet inside the barbed wire fence was a single wire supported about a foot off the ground. This wire was called the dead line. All prison compounds had this particular feature. The rule was that if you crossed this trip-wire, the guards in the tower could and would shoot you. One end of our building was filled with 3-tiered steel bunks with the same thin mattresses. The only other pieces of furniture were a couple of benches. There were two small stoves and we were given one small pail of coal each day for each stove. Needless to say, it was never warm in the building, especially since the winter of 1944/1945 was one of the coldest winters in memory. Water for the 80 or so men in this building was made available through only two cold water taps. The toilet facility was an open-air latrine that every so often had to be emptied by hand into a tank and then transported away. Thankfully, I never had that duty.'

Men of 423rd Infantry Regiment, 2nd Battalion, Company H, on burial detail in Stalag IXB, April 1945. *Left to right* (clockwise): E M Pretty, Carrie Robinson (hidden), Ray Johnston, Bill Lawson, Paul Trost, Lloyd Diehl.

Burial site, outside camp above Stalag IXB, 3 April 1945.

Stalag IIB, Duchenstadt, another camp used to house 106th Division men.

Brick factory at Duchenstadt where prisoners were employed, bombed by the RAF in March 1945.

Then came the tragic nights of 23 and 24 December, cold clear conditions, ideal for bombing. The RAF and USAAF decided to plaster Germany with one of their heaviest raids yet. At Limburg on the night of 23 December, flares were dropped over the prison compound and the men knew they were about to be bombed. A survivor said the bombing actually lasted about 15 minutes but 'it seemed like a lifetime.' When it was over, the prisoner-officers' barracks was a shambles, with 68 American officers killed and only four or five survivors. This bombing, said to have been by the RAF was one of those terrible needless tragedies of the war.

That same night a train was bombed whilst it stood in the marshalling yards of Koblenz. Many of the men died, hit by shrapnel which pierced the frail wooden box cars quite easily. One truck took a direct hit killing all its occupants. The bodies of the dead men were carried along for another two days before the train finally reached its destination.

John Kline managed to keep a diary, he had marched 110 miles from the point of capture on Hill 504 to the first prisoner transit camp, Stalag XII-A, at Limburg. Arriving there at 10.30 am on the 30 December. During his short stay at the camp he was given a large portion of bread, but no water. The men were then loaded onto the now infamous box cars for another journey to another camp. One of the occupants of his truck tied a can to some string and dragged it along the ground to collect snow for melting into drinking water. A large can was placed in the corner for sanitary purposes. Many of the men now had diarrhoea, and so the stench in the crowded truck was awful. This journey took seven days and six nights before arriving at Stalag IV-B near Muhlberg 7 January, 1945. Here they were finally given a shower and their clothes deloused. Sanitary conditions here were not much better than the train. On 10 January it was John's 20th birthday. He wrote in his diary,

Sergeant John Kline after PoW fare and a 525 mile walk.

> *'I am spending it as a guest of the German government at Stalag IV-B. I had 1/6th loaf of bread, one tablespoon sugar, one slice of margarine and a*

129

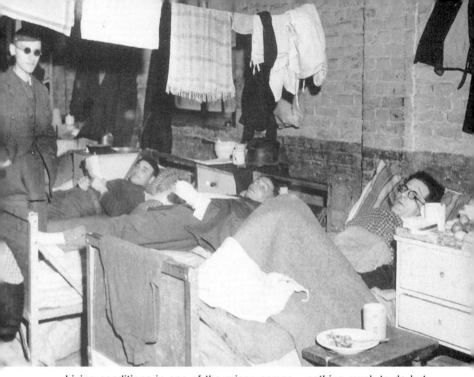

Living conditions in one of the prison camps – nothing much to do but wait for liberation as the Allied armies closed in on Nazi Germany.

Smiles all round – these 106th Division prisoners would soon be free.

THE BROT

Free at last! It's all over.

pint of grass soup with five boiled potatoes as a birthday meal.'

He spent only one week at Muhlberg before being shipped by train to Stalag VIII-A at Gorlitz about seventy miles northeast of Dresden on the Polish border. One month later he was on the move again. This time due to the advancing Russian troops. Valentine's Day, 14 February, the sixteen hundred Americans headed west. This time to the town of Duderstadt and the 'Brick Factory' camp. It was not an official 'Stammlager' (Prisoner of War Camp), but just a point where the Germans had decided to accumulate several thousand prisoners.

It was four stories in height with one narrow staircase. Each floor was piled high with clay bricks ready for the kiln.

From here the groups were split up. Some went north-west to Stalag XI-B at Fallingbostel. Or like John went north to a work camp at Braunschweig. By this time John was so weak he could not walk any more. He ended up being housed in a Farben Industries ammunition plant infirmary, in the town of Helmstedt.

At 10.30am on 13 April, 1945, he along with many other prisoners of war in that area were liberated by the American Army.

As a prisoner John Kline had actually walked over 525 miles.

Lieutenant-Colonel Riggs, of the 81st Engineer Combat Battalion also had an amazing story to tell. During the fight for St Vith, Riggs had been grazed on the head by a mortar fragment, knocking him unconscious. On coming to, he was surrounded by German soldiers, and taken to an assembly point where he was grouped with about forty other prisoners. He was then marched for twelve days into Germany. Now and then, the Germans would stop near a village to get food, throwing only the crusts from their sandwiches to the Americans. Riggs finally arrived at a prison camp, Stalag 4. It was not long before he found himself on the move again, this time on his own. Perhaps as punishment he thought, for only revealing his name and serial number. His new camp was in Poland. On going to the

Officers are freed.

PoWs from two different barracks two days after liberation, 2 April 1945.
The camp is Stalag IXB, Bad Orb, Germany.

106th officers after their liberation: medical officers, middle and far right; dentist second left; chaplains, left and second right.

106th medical staff at Stalag IXB, Bad Orb, photographs taken by liberation soldiers.

latrine one day he noticed that the usual guard was not there. Taking advantage of this he decided to escape. He got to a deserted dining hall and climbed on top of a large walk-in refrigerator and hid. His name was called at roll call and finding him missing the Germans started to search the camp, some with dogs. The German patrols came and went out of the dining hall, but no one thought of looking on top of the fridge. Come nightfall with no guards about he threw himself through a double roll of barbed wire and headed in the direction of Warsaw, which he knew the Russians had taken. Three nights later whilst hiding in a culvert he felt a tap on the shoulder. He explained the best he could to the stranger that had stumbled upon him that he was an American officer. The man threw his arms around him and kissed him on both cheeks – the Polish underground had found him. He was taken to a safe house and fed potatoes, sausage and warm milk. The underground took Riggs to a Russian colonel who said, 'Come on, Americanski, I'll have you in Berlin in a couple of weeks and you can meet your own people.' The promise was kept.

With Hitler's Third Reich in ruins, and that despotic dictator's war-machine utterly defeated, hundreds of thousands of perpetrators and victims of the 'New Order'

A mixed bag of freed prisoners start on the long road home.

Charles Paetschke's souvenirs of Stalag XIB: starting with mess kit used to hold the warm 'coffee' served as breakfast and the 'soup' in the evening. Camp 'dog tag', No. 23391, in front of newspaper. Newspaper and armband were taken by him in a quick visit to the camp HQ on the last day in camp. The stack of papers are the names of fellow prisoners plus all the names of foods and restaurants they were able to remember.

were on the move in Europe – heading home.

Also heading home were those men who had survived that relatively brief, yet brutal, ordeal after being taken prisoner in the Ardennes, in and around St Vith. Some would spend many months in hospital suffering with all kinds of diseases, nearly all had malnutrition. Yet they all held in common one binding factor – all were proud of being part of the 106th Infantry Division.

The 106th was reconstituted at Rheims, France. Here the Colour Detail of the 422nd and the 423rd Regiments parade.

CHAPTER SEVEN

TOURING THE BATTLEFIELD TODAY

First of all, your own transport is a must, there is no real public transport in the area that will go anywhere near the rural areas in which the battles took place. To get to this part of Europe it is best to drive. There are the airports in Brussels, Luxembourg and Cologne, but it would mean hiring a car from there.

From the ferry port of Ostende, take the main motorway number E40 and head for Brugge, Gent, Brussels, Liège. After Liège the signs will start indicating Aachen and Germany.

Turn right onto the E42, marked Verviers, Spa, eventually St Vith will be reached. Or, carry straight on looking out for a sign for Bleialf. You are now in the thick of it, as they say. There are many hotels and guest houses in the larger towns

St Vith Railway Station in 1945.

of St Vith and Prum, both within easy reach of the battlefields. Or, you can stay in any of the numerous 'Gasthaus' or smaller hotels scattered around the area. All villages have at least one. These are good value for money. Both St Vith and Prum have railway stations, the line to Bleialf is now closed.

Roads in the area are marked L: (Landes) = Country, K (Kreis) = County and B (Bundes) = National.

The people are very friendly on both sides of the border, each village no matter how small, seems to have a bar. Quite a pleasing site after scrambling around the rugged terrain. Just look for the 'Bit Burger' signs, an excellent local brew.

Most of the villages have been rebuilt since the war. The locals have a knack of blending the new with the old, so that it is difficult to distinguish between the two.

St Vith

The town was virtually flattened in December 1944, little now exists of the original town buildings, although the road lay-out still remains the same. As can be seen by the map drawn by a member of the 2nd Infantry Division on the 15/11/44, we can take it that, because the 106th relieved the 2nd, man for man, the various headquarters, motor pools etc would have been in the same positions, only the code words would have changed.

Approaching the centre of town from the north, a large crossroads will be found with a roundabout. Proceed straight across into Klosterstrasse and about a quarter of a mile on the right can be seen a monument dedicated to the 106th Infantry Division. This monument was erected by the 106th Infantry Division Association and is cared for by the people of St Vith. The building behind the flags was the original memorial which was built in the mid 50's. It is now being used by the school. In mid 1995 a new memorial was erected in front of the old. The large rock comes from the local region, and is special to that area. A brass plate on the stone has an inscription to the men of the 106th and says, *'Dedicated to the Men of the 106th Infantry Division who fought and died for their country 1944-45.'*

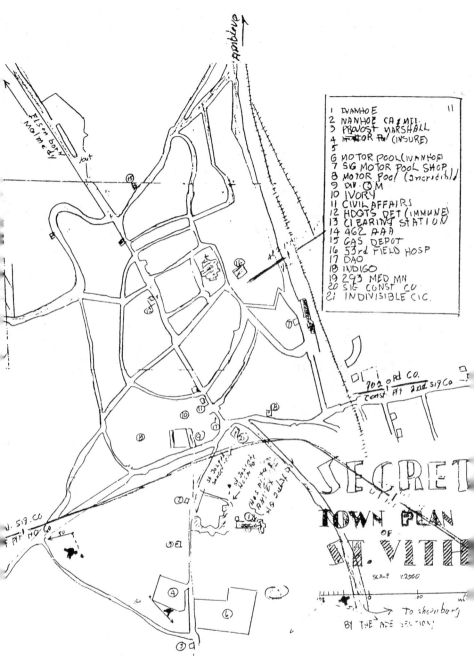

Map of St Vith drawn 15 November 1944. The
106th Infantry Division took over position for
position.

Monument to the 106th Infantry Division in St Vith.

This was the sight of Divisional Headquarters.

Come **back** to the crossroads and **turn right** on to the N26. On leaving St Vith the road twists and starts to climb into the forest. This area is the Prumerberg heights, scene of the desperate defence by Colonel Riggs and his Engineers. There is a memorial on the left **at the top** of the heights to the men of the Engineers. You can **park** by the side of the road and **walk into the woods**, either left or right, much evidence can be seen of the fighting that took place here between the 17 – 21 December.

A word of warning here. Munitions are still lying about and are very dangerous, be careful what you pick-up. Digging or metal detecting is not encouraged, in fact it is forbidden. If in doubt about anything lying around, DO NOT TOUCH. This goes for the entire battleground. Rejoin your car.

Moving along the Schonberg road towards Heuem (81st Combat Engineers HQ) look out for a decorative wrought iron works on the right, immediately **opposite** there is a small road north, on the left hand side. This road leads through the dense forest, eventually coming out at the village of Meyerode. About **500 yards** up this road is a small monument on the left, tucked into the trees. It is a simple, inscribed cross, the monument was erected by the people of Meyerode in honour of Lieutenant Eric Fisher Wood of the 589th Field Artillery Battalion. His body was found nearby. He is now buried in the American War Cemetery at Henri Chapelle.

If you stay on this small road and get to Meyerode, there in the village outside the school is a German 75mm anti-tank gun. Opposite the school is a bar, this was once Dietrich's Headquarters for a time. You can get back on track by **turning right in the village**, and heading towards Wereth and Herresbach. Just after Wereth, on the left at the edge of a field is a newly erected monument, this was

Shells, bits of half-track found at the base of Lindscheid Hill.

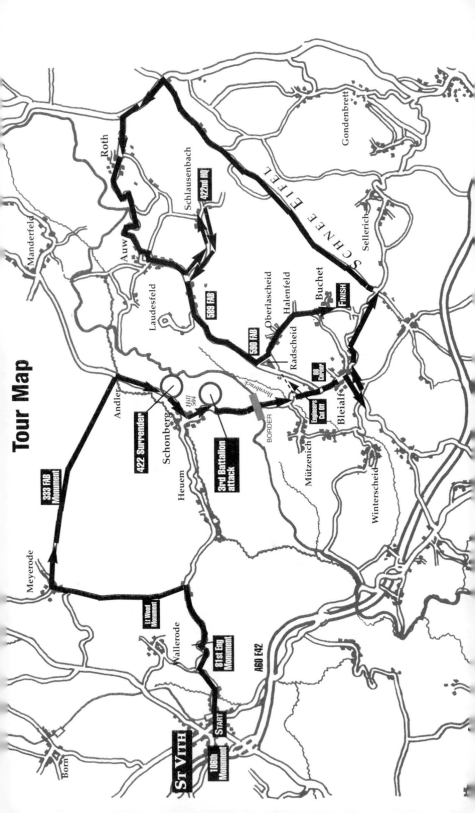

Tour Map

ST VITH

106th Monument

START

81st Eng Monument

A60 E42

Wallerode

Lt Wood Monument

Meyerode

Born

333 FAB Monument

Andler

Schonberg

422 Surrender

Hill 504

Heuem

3rd Battalion attack

Ihrenbruck

BORDER

Mützenich

Winterscheid

Engineers Cut Off

Bleialf

BG Cavender

Radscheid

590 FAB

Oberlascheid

Halenfeld

Buchet

FINISH

589 FAB

Laudesfeld

Auw

422nd HQ

Schlausenbach

Roth

Manderfeld

SCHNEE EIFEL

Gondenbrett

Sellerich

erected in honour of the eleven black soldiers of the 333rd Field Artillery Battalion, a Corps artillery battalion attached to the 106th, who were murdered by the SS. Carry on to Andler. In Andler there is the inevitable bar, Gasthaus Kessler. In this building was housed Company A, 331st Medical Battalion, serving the 422nd Infantry Regiment and the 14th Cavalry, it was used as their Aid Station. Opposite, there used to be a dance hall, owned by Herr Kessler, captured American Officers were brought for interrogation. The famous photographs and propaganda German newsreel film of American prisoners being marched away was filmed alongside the River Our in this vicinity.

From Andler proceed **back down the N26** towards Schonberg. About **half a mile on the left** is another small road which forks off the N26. If you look up the open slope to the top of the hill, you will see where the 422nd Infantry came out of the woods and saw below them (where you are) vehicles 'bumper to bumper', the occupants of which then proceeded to open fire on them. You can **drive or walk up this fork road**, which will lead you to the spot where the remnants of the 422nd surrendered. It is in the area where the road ends and leads into a track passing through the woods.

Into Schonberg, this is another place that has been rebuilt, even the bridge across the Our River is in a slightly different location. Turn left in Schonberg and the road starts to climb steeply. The large hill on the left, covered in trees, is the famous Hill 504. Where the road (N595) does a large left hand loop there is a **lay-by on the right**.

Looking up the road, there is a logging trail up on the left. Down that trail came men from Klinck's 3rd Battalion, Company L and met the American Sherman tank manned by Germans. Heavy fighting took place on this spot. Both sides of the road were littered with German and American dead. The 3rd Battalion, what was left of it, was pulled back up the trail to the top. It was here that Cavender joined them and finally gave the order for the 423rd to surrender.

There is still much to see on the top of the hill, numerous

foxholes and shell craters. But once again, please be careful as there is still a lot of live ammunition kicking about.

Proceed south, all the woods on the left were held by the 106th, and attached VIII Corps Artillery units, you do not have to walk far anywhere along this road to find the evidence. Large pits dug into the ground, which once were the emplacements for artillery pieces such as 155mm and 8 inch howitzers. The place is littered with the clover leaf shaped trays that once were containers for shells and powder charges, and the lifting eyes for the shells are in abundance everywhere. As you come out of the woods there is a **turning right** that leads to Amelscheid, immediately opposite this in the open field, was the final position of the 589th Field Artillery Battalion, before it drove 'hell for leather' through Schonberg and some of it onto St Vith. Also, it was on this part of the road that the unsuspecting German Volkswagen fell into line with the convoy of M8 armoured cars, and was consequently shot to bits. Midway down the hill, you will pass from Belgium into Germany; there is a small (usually unmanned) customs post on your right. At the bottom is the hamlet of Ihrenbruck. Just before the large old custom house on the right, is a patch of woods, here was stationed Service Battery of the 589th FAB. Follow the road **across the bridge** of the Ihrenbach stream – it starts to climb again. At the very sharp bend half way up the hill is a **trail on the left**. This was cut through the woods and became the entrance to 'Engineers Cut-Off'. Remains of the couduroy road can still be seen in places. Continue on the main road, follow it to the **top of the hill** where it comes out on a curve. This area is called Justenschlag. But to the GIs, it was named '88 Corner' or 'Purple Heart Corner'. Left is 'Skyline Drive', right and down the hill is Bleialf. As you can imagine, any movement in this vicinity, could easily be observed from the German positions in and around Brandscheid, far on the horizon directly south. The high wooded mass south and to the left of Brandscheid is the Schnee Eifel.

Proceed down the hill into the town of Bleialf.

Village of Bleialf where the heaviest fighting in the St Vith sector took place – then and now.

Here there are still some original old buildings dotted about, but, as with the rest of the area, it took its share of destruction. In the centre is the Church, it was around this, that there was particularly vicious fighting those first few days. When the local priest emerged after the initial battle bodies were strewn everywhere, both American and German. After the mass surrender the majority of American prisoners spent their first night in the ground of this Church, before being marched off deeper into Germany. The famous American author Kurt Vonnegut was one such prisoner that passed through here. Later as a prisoner of war he witnessed the destruction of Dresden by Allied bombers. This later went on to inspire him to write the classic novel *Slaughterhouse Five*. Ernest Hemingway also was here. He had a meal in the cafe/bar opposite (Cafe Zwicker). But this was slightly earlier, when the American 4th Division initially captured Bleialf. He was with Officers, members of this Division, his favourite, whom he tagged along with. Apparently he spent the entire time complaining because of the noise from a field artillery battalion firing from dug-in positions behind the bar. In the town are a couple of small, but well stocked supermarkets, plus an excellent bakery and butchers. A small tip, because of the rural nature of the area, very very few people speak English, so if you don't 'sprechen Deutsch' take a good phrase book with you. Also there, is a petrol station, where somebody will serve you, chat about the weather and give the kids a sweet whilst they fill you up.

Drive south-west out of town for about one mile and you will see what used to be Bleialf railway station. It is now a private house. Viewing south from this point, you will see where the main effort of the German attack came from, in their final onslaught to take Bleialf on 17 December. If you **follow this road** it will take you into the area of the other 106th Division regiment the 424th. Come **back** into Bleialf and pass the **Church on your left**, follow the road out and round until you come to a **cross roads** at the foot of the Schnee Eifel. By the side of the road is a bus shelter with a small parking area. This area was being held by Company A, 423rd Infantry, on the morning of 16 December. **Stand in front** of the shelter and look forward into the forest; you are viewing the area held by Company B. The road that goes right leads to Brandscheid, a village held at that time by the Germans. It became known as 'Little Verdun', because it was captured and retaken so many times during the conflict. It was a difficult place to take, owing to the many fortifications, for it was an intregal part of the West Wall or Siegfried Line.

Straight on will take you to Sellerich and eventually Prum.

Schnee Eifel. Company B, 423rd Infantry Regiment positions were in the woods to the right.

This was the way the 18th Volksgrenadier Division came in their attack on the southerly pincer move around the Schnee Eifel. Left is signposted Schwarzer Mann, or as the Americans called it, 'Bogeyman Hill'. This is the start of the famed Schnee Eifel. Unless you visit the area in the depth of winter when there is two or three foot of snow on the ground and the temperature is well below freezing you cannot start to imagine how much the men suffered. Now all is calm, the stately fir trees give welcome shade from the sun, but even now, standing alone next to a front line foxhole, starts the mind racing on how it must have been. In the centre of the ridge is the Schwarzer Mann, the highest spot around. There is a bar/restaurant there, and in the winter the area is used for snow sports. This spot just about marks the boundary between the 422nd and the 423rd. Bunkers are abundant left and right of the road. This main tarmac road was not there during the war, but the unimproved trail to the left was then the main access. Hence the bunker line alongside of it. The majority of these bunkers, not destroyed during the conflict, were finally blown by the French in 1949.

The actual front-line foxholes of the infantrymen, are in the woods to the right of the road, about 300 to 400 yards on the forward slope. Many are still in evidence. Great care must be taken when parking, not to block the trails, these are not in constant use, but farmers or loggers have a nasty habit of creeping up on you and get fed up if they cannot get by. During summer, needless to say, everywhere dries out, so fire is a big risk. Smoking in the forest is 'Verboten'. There is nothing dangerous lurking, apart from the odd wild boar, who can turn funny if disturbed or upset.

On reaching the end of the Schnee Eifel, **turn left** on the B265 and travel for a short distance, turn **left again** and head for the villages of Roth and Auw. This is the southern end of the Losheim Gap. Many German units came this way during the attack. **In Auw turn left** again by the Church. This spot was where the Germans started nosing up the hill towards the 589th FAB. This road was called 'Skyline Drive' or 'Skyline Boulevard' by the Americans. Proceed **up this road, first left** will take you to Schlausenbach; Descheneaux of the 422nd had his headquarters in the Inn here. You cannot go any further by car. Walking the many tracks will take you back up to the Schnee Eifel.

Retrace your steps and come back up to 'Skyline Drive', **turn left**. About one hundred yards was where the 589th FAB had its outpost on 16 December. Drive into the tiny hamlet of Herzfenn; the 589th FAB were based in and around here. Battery B and C were to the right and just inside the tree line, Battery A was to the left and on the edge of a patch of woods just under half a mile away. See location map of 589th FAB for more details. **Turning right** immediately at the far end of the hamlet, will take you to the village of Laudesfeld where the 592nd FAB with its 155mm howitzers was emplaced. Just south-west of Laudesfeld a high hill will be observed, in this area on 19 December, approximately 500 men from all different units made a perimeter defence, and held on until finally surrendering on the morning of 21 December, 1944.

The next hamlet along 'Skyline Drive' is Radscheid. Here the 590th Field Artillery Battalion were in position,

View from Skyline Drive looking south.

with its firing batteries in the woods on the left of the road. Leaving the car here, by two solitary buildings one of which was the 590th headquarters, you can **walk to the right**, down a farm track, passing open fields, and into the woods. This track was used by the 423rd Regiment and 590th FAB on their way to attack Schonberg. At the end of the track another will be found running parallel to the Ihrenbach stream, **turn right and follow the track** until you come across a clearing. Across the stream is a small wooden bridge. The 423rd Infantry crossed here, on its way to Hill 504.

The aid station was in scrub undergrowth just across the stream. This whole area was jammed with vehicles from the regiment, unable to cross the boggy ground. Also here, was the 590th FAB which had only just set-up. The Germans overran this position at about 0930 on 19 December. It was here that we found 105mm ammunition in evidence and numerous hastily dug foxholes, ammunition boxes etc.

Cross the stream and head off up the hill. The 1st and 2nd Battalions were here behind Hill 536 at daybreak on 19 December. It is where Cavender gave the orders to

Foxholes and debris of battle on Hill 504. Typical of the sort of rusting artifacts to be discovered throughout the area of the Battle of the Bulge.

attack Schonberg and was immediately hit by an artillery bombardment. Moving on will eventually bring you to Hill 504. It's quite a walk!

Return to 'Skyline Drive', **turn left** into the village of Radscheid, Oberlascheid, Halenfeld and Buchet, where Cavender had his headquarters. Continuing through, you will come back out onto the main road between Bleialf and the Schnee Eifel. **Turn right** for Bleialf. It is possible to stop alongside any forest area in the region, and only after a short walk into the woods find evidence of fighting. This is because the area was fought over for quite a long time, and many units passed through during the conflict from September 1944 to the beginning of February 1945.

There are two really good museums that are worth a visit but are about an hour's drive away. One is at La Gleize, the furthest point Kampfgruppe Peiper reached in the attack. Outside the museum is one of his Tiger II tanks left there after the Germans retreated. The other museum is at La Roche-en-Ardenne, dedicated to the Battle of the Bulge. In Vielsam, there is a Sherman tank in memory of the 7th Armored Division, and at Baraque Fraiture, also known as Parkers Crossroads, where Major Arthur C Parker III, along with remnants of Battery A 589th FAB and other units, set up their three remaining howitzers and made a roadblock. They were successful in holding up the 2nd SS Panzer Division and 560th Volksgrenadiers Division long enough to enable the 82nd Airborne to get into position. They were eventually overrun. To mark the spot there is a memorial with a 105mm Howitzer in position.

At Spineux (Wanne), in the centre of the village there is a monument dedicated to the men of the 424th Infantry Regiment of the 106th Infantry Division and also to the men of the 112th Regiment of the 28th Infantry Division. These two regiments survived the initial onslaught in December, and joined together to form a Combat Team which went on to push the Germans back. They subsequently liberated this local area in January 1945.

Enjoy your break or holiday in this part of the Ardennes, the scenery is breath-taking. Be prepared to do a lot of walking over rough terrain, so dress accordingly.

Above all try and cast your mind back to that terrible December in 1944 and give your respect to those brave soldiers of both sides.

Some further good reading on the subject:
A Time for Trumpets by Charles B MacDonald
St Vith, Lion in the Way by Colonel R Ernest Dupuy, reprinted by The Battery Press, INC, 1986
The Official Divisional History
Last Assault by Charles Whiting, Leo Cooper, 1994
Healing the Child Warrior by Richard W Peterson Ph.d (A member of the 106th Division)
U.S. Army in World War II The Ardennes, Battle of the Bulge by Hugh M. Cole, Deputy Theater Historian, European Theater of Operations, U.S. Army

Monument to the Combat Engineers on the Prumerberg Heights.

Memorial to Lieutenant Eric Fisher Wood (see page 85)

The view John Kline had of Schonberg from his 30 cal machine gun position.

Men of the 3rd Battalion 423rd Infantry Regiment came down the track onto the road on their ill-fated attack on Schonberg.

Company L, 3rd Battalion, 423rd Infantry Regiment, came onto the Schonberg road at this point and met the captured Sherman tank, which opened fire on them (see page 108).

The logging trail used by 3rd Battalion 423rd Infantry Regiment.

It was in this area by the Ihrenbach Stream that vehicles of 423rd Infantry Regiment and the 590th Field Artillery Battalion finally ended up.

Hastily dug foxholes and the remains of a 50 calibre ammunition box near the Ihrenbach Stream.

Andler-Schonberg Road, viewed from Andler. It was down this stretch of road that the right-hand pincer arm of the 18th Volksgrenadier Regiment advanced on the 17th December.

The author, Michael Tolhurst, with his two sons Stuart and Stevie in 1992 on the border bridge over the River Our, which marks the boundary between Belgium and Germany.

INDEX